A PREACHER GIRL'S SWORD OF THE SPIRIT

The earth was void and darkness covered the deep. Nothing changed in this darkness until God spoke into it, and nothing is going to change in your darkness until you learn to

SPEAK INTO IT!

Barbie Brown Glunt

ISBN 978-1-7366825-2-4 (Paperback)
ISBN 978-1-7366825-3-1 (Digital)

Copyright 2021 by Barbie Brown Glunt

All rights reserved. No part of this publication may be reproduced, distributed, or transmitted in any form or by any means, including photocopying, recording, or other electronic or mechanical methods without the prior written permission of the publisher. For permission requests, solicit the publisher via the address below.

Double Bar B Publishing
207 Hill Farm Road
Dunbar Pa 15431
Barbaraann777@zoominternet.net
Printed in the United States of America

DEDICATION

This book is dedicated to all the families that have suffered loss of a love one and/or endured the many trials and pain of seeing their love ones go through the agonizing grips of addiction and bondage.

Know that there is a way out through the Lord Jesus Christ. They can be set free!

ACKNOWLEDGMENTS

With sincere appreciation, I would like to thank Maryann Lilliock-Evans for being my special prayer partner and associate editor of 'A Preacher Girl's Sword of the Spirit.' Your insight and editorial knowledge was priceless.

I would also like to thank my dear designer, Diana Buidoso for creating a dynamic cover for this book. Your designing skills are among the best! Your patience and editorial skills were also much appreciated. God Bless you both!

CONTENTS

1. The Battle Line is Drawn 9
2. Areas of Temptation 19
3. Have No Other gods before Me 27
4. The Ministry of Jesus 37
5. The Keys of the Kingdom 47
6. Armor of God 53
7. Putting on the Helmet of Salvation 57
8. Putting on the Belt of Truth 65
9. Breast Plate of Righteousness 69
10. Shod your Feet with the Preparation 73
11. Taking up the Shield of Faith 79
12. Weapons of Warfare 85
13. Total Submission: Love and Obed 89
14. Prayer and Fasting 97
15. Baptism of the Holy Spirit 105
16. Praise 113
17. Speaking into your Darkness 119
18. It is the Spoken Word 127
19. Engaging the Battle Faith 143
20. A Stone and a Sling 155
21. The Three Heavens 167
22. Return to your First Love 173
23. Bible Studies Answers 177

PREFACE

The earth was void and darkness covered the deep. Nothing changed in this darkness until God spoke into it, and nothing is going to change in your darkness until you learn to

SPEAK INTO IT!

Jesus gave us everything we need in His Word to have a victorious life. But why are so many Christians defeated and in bondage? How determined are you to triumph over the darkness? Jesus and His angels are on stand-by waiting for someone to

ENGAGE THE BATTLE.

ARE YOU READY TO MOUNT UP?

CHAPTER 1

THE BATTLE LINE IS DRAWN

Genesis 1:1-3
New King James Version

In the beginning God created the heavens and the earth. The earth was without form, and void; and darkness was on the face of the deep. And the Spirit of God was hovering over the face of the waters. Then God said, "Let there be light"; and there was light. And God saw the light, that it was good; and God divided the light from the darkness. God called the light Day, and the darkness He called Night. So the evening and the morning were the first day. God goes on and calls forth the heavens, the sun, the moon, the earth, the seas, the grass, the herbs, the trees, animals, sea creatures, the birds and man.

Reading from **Genesis 1:31: Then God saw everything that He had made, and indeed it was very good. So the evening and the morning were the sixth day.** God saw everything that He made. He looked everything over and came up with one conclusion; it was good! He was pleased with His creation. He was pleased with the works of His hands. *It was good indeed!*

God spoke everything in existence by His spoken word. His word is life. As stated in **Hebrews chapter 4:12 For the word of God is living and powerful, and sharper than any two-edged sword, piercing even to the division of soul and spirit, and of the joints and marrow, and is a discerner of the thoughts and intents of the heart.** His word is living and powerful! Everything had life; the plants, the animals and man. There was no death in this beautiful creation world. Nothing could die. We had life, plants had life and animals had life. *No death!* It was a paradise. The birds were singing, the breeze was blowing and man was enjoying all the beautiful trees, animals and life in this creation.

We didn't have to do work. We were supposed to tend to the garden, not till it. God made everything perfect for us.

Nothing happened in this realm, until God spoke His word into it. **And nothing is going to happen in your darkness until you begin to speak into it!** *The same Spirit that brought life to a cold dark point in the universe, is the same Spirit that is in each of us that know Jesus.* Speak God's word into your darkness and see what happens. We will address this in more detail in a later chapter.

But higher on His agenda, more prominent on His mind, He wondered if man would not only appreciate what He had created for him, but would appreciate Him...... for who He is? Would man give Him the honor due to Him, seeing how He was the Lord and the Creator of all things. Would man obey His voice?

Reading from **Genesis 2:8,9 The Lord God planted a garden eastward in Eden, and there He put the man whom He had formed. And out of the ground the Lord God made every tree grow that is pleasant to the sight and good for food.**

The tree of life was also in the midst of the garden, and the tree of the knowledge of good and evil.

Then the command came. Reading from **Genesis 2:15 Then the Lord God took the man and put him in the garden of Eden to tend and keep it. And the Lord God commanded the man, saying, "Of every tree of the garden you may freely eat; but of the tree of the knowledge of good and evil you shall not eat, for in the day that you eat of it you shall surely die."**

Reading in chapter 3 of Genesis, we read that the serpent was more cunning than any beast of the field. The Bible refers the serpent to a beast of the field. So originally the serpent was some kind of beast. When we see the word serpent we automatically think of a snake. But that didn't happen to this mammal until after the fall of man.

The serpent poses a question to Eve, by asking her, if God told her that she should not eat of every tree of the garden? Eve answers by saying, **Genesis 3:2 "We may eat the fruit of the trees of the garden; but of the fruit of the tree which is in the midst of the garden, God has**

said, 'You shall not eat it, nor shall you touch it, lest you die.'"

Now the lie from the serpent. Reading **from Genesis 3:4,5 Then the serpent said to the woman, "You will not surely die. For God knows that in the day you eat of it your eyes will be opened, and you will be like God, knowing good and evil."** The serpent tells Eve a lie, that she will not surely die, and then he tells her a truth that her eyes will be open and she will be like God.

So why couldn't man eat from the tree of knowledge of good and evil? Because, he could eat from every tree in the garden which included the tree of life, (because man had life), if he ate also from the tree of knowledge of good and evil, he would be like God; having both life and knowledge.

Genesis 3:6,7 So when the woman saw that the tree was good for food, that it was pleasant to the eyes, and a tree desirable to make one wise, she took of its fruit and ate. She also gave to her husband with her, and he ate. Then the eyes of both of them were opened, and they knew that they were naked; and they sewed fig leaves together and made themselves coverings.

The same areas of temptation that the serpent tempted Eve in are the same areas of temptation that he tempted Jesus in, are the same areas of temptation that the devil tempts mankind in daily. **Lust of the flesh**, the woman saw that the tree was good for food. **Lust of the eyes**, that it was pleasant for the eyes. **Pride of life**, a tree desirable to make one wise.

The Bible says their eyes were opened, and they knew they were naked. To cover up their nakedness they sewed fig leaves together and made coverings for themselves.

What they didn't realize was that because of their disobedience, sin had now entered in. The consequences of sin…is death. Now man had lost his life, plants lost their lives and animals lost their lives. The fig leaves that they sewed together would now die and dry up. And the leaves would not cover their nakedness. The only thing that could cover them would be the tunics of skin that the Lord God made for them. Therefore, if the Lord God made them tunics of skin, an animal had to die; which meant blood had to be spilled. A sacrifice had to be made for their sin. Not only did a sacrifice have to be made, but the consequences of that sin would be the fall of all creation through curses. *So there is always a price that must be paid for sin. You never get away with it.* **Romans 6:23 For the wages of sin is death, but the gift of God is eternal life in Christ Jesus our Lord.**

The serpent is now cursed more than all cattle and every beast of the field. He would go on his belly and eat dust all the days of his life. The Lord will greatly multiply the women's sorrow and conception and in pain she shall bring forth children.

Her desire would be for her husband and he shall rule over her. And the ground would be cursed for the man, in toil he shall eat from it all the days of his life. It would bring forth thorns and thistles and in the sweat of his face he shall eat bread. Through all of these curses, the Lord God gives mankind a glimmer of hope. A glimmer of hope that would span generations, religions, ideologies and prophecies, until eternity!

That glimmer is found when the Lord is cursing the serpent. He says in **Genesis 3:15 "And I will put enmity Between you and the woman, and between your seed and her Seed; He shall bruise your head, and you shall bruise His heel."** The battle line is now drawn. The serpent, aka Satan, would now be our enemy. The serpent's seed would now be enemies with the woman' seed. Jesus would come from a woman. He would be the seed from the woman. But the good news is the rest of that sentence. He shall bruise your head. Jesus shall bruise the head of the serpent, but he, the serpent, shall bruise His heel. The serpent might get his blows in and bruise Jesus's heel but Jesus gets the ultimate victory for He would bruise his head.

Jesus is speaking, **Luke 10:18 "I saw Satan fall like lightning from heaven. Behold, I give you the authority to trample on serpents and scorpions, and over all the power of the enemy, and nothing shall by any means hurt you. Nevertheless do not rejoice in this, that the spirits are subject to you, but rather rejoice because your names are written in heaven."**

The battle line is drawn and the outcome of the battle is already established. Jesus wins! And those who are following Jesus wins! Thank God for His glimmer of hope, Jesus!

Chapter 1 Bible Study

1. How did God create the heavens and the earth?

2. What was the name of the tree that Adam and Eve was commanded not to eat of?

3. True or False: The snake in Chapter 3 of Genesis was a reptile?

4. If man ate from the Tree of Life and the Tree of knowledge of good and evil, he would be like_____.

5. Name the three areas of temptation that Satan tempted Eve in?

6. Why couldn't the fig leaves cover Adam and Eve?

7. When God made Adam and Eve tunics from animal skins what sacrifice had to be made?

8. In Genesis 3:15 Who would be the one to bruise Satan's head?

CHAPTER 2

AREAS OF TEMPTATION

These same areas of temptation that Satan tempted Eve in, are the same areas that Satan tempts us with today; the lust of the flesh; Eve saw that the tree was good for food, the lust of the eyes; it was pleasant to the eyes, and the pride of life; a tree desirable to make one wise, the pride of life. They are also the same areas that Satan tempted Jesus in **Matthew chapter 4:1-11**, but Jesus gets the victory over Satan by quoting God's word back to him.

When the tempter came to Jesus he said, **"If You are the Son of God, command that these stones become bread." But he answered and said, "It is written, 'Man shall not live by bread alone, but by every word that proceeds from the mouth of God.'"** This area of temptation is lust of the flesh, because Jesus fasted 40 days and nights and was hungry. The devil tries to appeal to Jesus by having Him prove His deity, but Jesus responds with the word of God.

Then the devil sets Him on the pinnacle of a temple and says to Him, **"If You are the Son of God, throw Yourself down. For it is written: 'He shall give His angels charge over you,' and, 'in their hands they shall bear you up, Lest you dash your foot against a stone.'"**

Jesus said to him, "It is written again, 'You shall not tempt the Lord your God.'" This area of temptation is pride of life. Now the devil uses God's word to try and tempt Jesus. And Jesus responds with another scripture to counter Satan. ***This is why it is so important to know the Bible in its entirety.*** The devil will try to tempt us with half-truths. We must know the complete word of God!

Then the devil takes Jesus up on a high mountain and showed Him all the kingdoms of the world and their glory. And he said to Him, **"All these things I will give You if You will fall down and worship me."**

Then Jesus said to him, "Away with you, Satan! For it is written, 'You shall worship the Lord your God, and Him only you shall serve.'"

This area of temptation is the lust of the eyes; for Satan showed Him all the kingdoms of the world and their glory. Here we see where Satan's real motives lie. Satan wants to be worshipped. He wants people to bow before him. He wants to be like God.

Reading from **1 John 2:15 Do not love the world or the things in the world. If anyone loves the world, the love of the Father is not in him. For all that is in the world----the lust of the flesh, the lust of the eyes, and the pride of life----is not of the Father but is of the world. And the world is passing away, and the lust of it; but he who does the will of God abides forever.**

Eve gave in to the temptation and all of humanity fell. Jesus showed us how to defeat Satan with the word of God *in its entirety*. Remember the devil knows the word of God, but he will twist it or only give you a half truth. That is why it is so important to read your Bible and hide God's word in your heart. Study to show yourself approved by God, as it says in **2 Tim 2:15 Be diligent to present yourself approved to God, a worker who does not need to be ashamed, rightly dividing the word of truth."**

Know the Bible inside and out; in its entirety, so when the tempter comes to you, you will have the ability to speak out God's word in complete truth and defeat the enemy. ***There is nothing more powerful than the word of God and knowing it ......in its entirety.***

CHOOSE THIS DAY WHOM YOU WILL SERVE

Now that the battle line is drawn, the real question is, what side do you want to be on? The Lord always gives His people a choice. He is a just and upright God. He would *never* 'make' us serve Him, what kind of pleasure would he get out of that? If He wanted robots, He could make them anytime. No, He is a God who deals with the heart. He is looking for a people who wants to serve Him, wants to trust Him, wants to love Him and wants to obey Him; knowing that He has our best interests in mind. He deals with the heart of man.

John 3:16 For God so loved the world that He gave His only begotten Son, that whoever believes in Him should not perish but have everlasting life. For God did not send His Son into the world to condemn the world, but that the world through Him might be saved.

"He who believes in Him is not condemned; but he who does not believe is condemned already, because he has not believed in the name of the only begotten Son of God.

And this is the condemnation, that the light has come into the world, and men loved darkness rather than light because their deeds were evil.

For everyone practicing evil hates the light and does not come to the light, lest his deeds should be exposed.

But he who does the truth comes to the light, that his deeds may be clearly seen, that they have been done in God."

Men who love darkness rather than light will condemn themselves, because their deeds are evil. The Lord gives everyone an opportunity to come to the light and be saved. Those who reject His love, reject His salvation and therefore chooses to be condemned.

Chapter 2 Bible Study:

1. How did Jesus get the victory over Satan's temptations?

2. Why must we know the complete word of God?

3. What is Satan's real motives?

4. Who will abide forever in 1 John 2:15?

5. What is the first step to have eternal life?

6. What is the condemnation?

CHAPTER 3

HAVE NO OTHER GODS BEFORE ME

The first four commandments in **Exodus 20:1-6** says this, **And God spoke all these words,** saying: "I am the Lord your God, who brought you out of the land of Egypt, out of the house of bondage.

"You shall have no other gods before Me.

"You shall not make for yourself any carved image, or any likeness of anything that is in heaven above, or that is in the earth beneath, or that is in the water under the earth; you shall not bow down to them nor serve them. For I, the Lord your God, am a jealous God, visiting the iniquity of the fathers on the children to the third and fourth generations of those who hate Me, but showing mercy to thousands, to those who love Me and keep My commandments.

"You shall not take the name of the Lord your God in vain, for the Lord will not hold him guiltless who takes His name in vain.

"Remember the Sabbath day, to keep it holy. Six days you shall labor and do all your work, but the seventh day is the Sabbath of the Lord your God. In it you shall do no work:

You might say, well this doesn't concern me for I don't carve any images or statues and bow down before them. I don't serve any other gods. So, I'm good. Well, let's look at the word 'god'. The definition for the word 'god' in Webster's New World Dictionary is:

1. Any of various beings conceived of as supernatural, immortal, and having special powers over people and nature; esp., a male deity.

2. An image that is worshipped; idol.

3. A person or thing deified or excessively honored and admired.

4. The creator and ruler of the universe, eternal, all powerful, and all-knowing; Supreme Being; Almighty.

If the Lord is God, and He is a good God, then He has a responsibility as God to provide, protect and meet the needs of His people. Each one of us need to ask ourselves some questions. Who, or what are we going to, to meet our needs? Are we looking for a quick fix to make us feel good by looking to drugs, alcohol, tobacco, sexual immorality etc.? If we are, **then they become our gods!** Are we searching out mediums, seances and ouija boards for fortunetelling, **then they become our gods!** Are we spending most of our time idolizing the latest singer, dancer or actor and listening to their music or watching their movies, **then they become our gods!** What or whomever takes your time, your devotion, your energy, your finances and your love become your gods.

The Lord says He is a jealous God. **He will not take second place to anyone or anything.** He wants to be number one in your life. He wants your love, your devotion, your worship.

Isn't it nice to know that He is for us and loves us. He wants us! *He says to have no other gods before Him! What He says He means.*

When the rich young ruler wanted to know what good thing he shall do so that he may have eternal life, Jesus told him to keep the commandments. Reading from **Matthew 19:18-22 He said to Him, "Which ones?" Jesus said, "'You shall not murder,' 'You shall not commit adultery,' 'You shall not steal,' 'You shall not bear false witness,' 'Honor your father and your mother,' and, 'You shall love your neighbor as yourself.'" The young man said to him, "All these things I have kept from my youth. What do I still lack?" Jesus said to him, "If you want to be perfect, go, sell what you have and give to the poor, and you will have treasure in heaven; and come, follow Me."** But when the young man heard that saying, he went away sorrowful, for he had great possessions.

Jesus only quoted the last six commandments to him for he had already broken the first four, for his riches were before the Lord.

Kingdom living is about relationships; our relationship with the Lord, and our relationship with other people. The first four commandments has to do with our relationship with the Lord:

1. Have no other gods before Him

2. Do not make a graven image and bow down before it.

3. Do not take the name of the Lord thy God in vain.

4. Remember the Sabbath to keep it holy.

    The last six commandments have to do with our relationship with other people.

5. Honor your father and your mother

6. You shall not murder

7. You shall not commit adultery

8. You shall not steal

9. You shall not bear false witness against neighbor.

10.   You shall not covet anything that is your neighbor's.

But what is critical, is that our relation ships have to be in the right order! The Lord has to be our first love! With Him first in our life, everything else will fall into place.

When one of the Pharisees questioned Jesus in **Matthew 22:36-40** He said, **"Teacher, which is the great commandment in the law?" Jesus said to him, "'You shall love the Lord your God with all your heart, with all your soul, and with all your mind.' This is the first and great commandment. And the second is like it; 'You shall love your neighbor as yourself.' On these two commandments hang all the Law and the Prophets."** So, in obeying these two commandments and *keeping them in the right order*, we are fulfilling all the law and doing everything the prophets had instructed. In other words, keeping these two commandments and keeping them in the right order, we are on our way to heaven!

Jesus speaking in **Matthew 10:37-39 He who loves father or mother more than Me is not worthy of Me. And he who loves son or daughter more than Me is not worthy of Me. And he who does not take his cross and follow after Me is not worthy of Me. He who finds his life will lose it, and he who loses his life for My sake will find it.**

Reading from **1 Timothy 2:5 For there is one God and one Mediator between God and men, the Man Christ Jesus**. A mediator is a person who speaks on our behalf. Jesus is the **only** mediator between us and God because He is the one who died for us. No one else has the privilege to mediate for us, for no one else paid the ultimate price and shed their blood to make a way for us. That is why Jesus said, **John 14:6 "I am the way, the truth, and the life. No one comes to the Father except through me."** If you are praying to someone or something else to intercede for you; a saint, a person, an idol, Mary; then you are having another god before the Lord.

Jesus is the only mediator between God and men. Pray to Him. Nowhere in the Bible does it say to pray to another person.

In fact, Jesus says He and the Father are one. And He says to pray to the Father and whatever we ask in Jesus' name it will be given to us.

Chapter 3 Bible Study:

1. The first four commandments are about what relationships?

2. If the Lord is our God, what is He responsible for?

3. Why did Jesus only quote the last six commandments to the rich young ruler?

4. What is the most critical principal about our relationships?

5. Name the Great Commandment.

6. Name the second Great Commandment.

7. Who is the mediator between God and man?

8. How can one come to the Father?

CHAPTER 4

The Ministry of Jesus

Reading form **Matthew 1:18 Now the birth of Jesus Christ was as follows: After His mother Mary was betrothed to Joseph, before they came together, she was found with child of the Holy Spirit. Then Joseph her husband, being a just man, and not wanting to make her a public example, was minded to put her away secretly. But while he thought about these things, behold an angel of the Lord appeared to him in a dream, saying, "Joseph, son of David, do not be afraid to take to you Mary your wife, for that which is conceived in her is of the Holy Spirit. And she will bring forth a Son, and you shall call His name JESUS, for He will save His people from their sins."**

So all this was done that it might be fulfilled which was spoken by the Lord through the prophet, saying: *"Behold, the virgin shall be with child, and bear a Son, and they shall call His name Immanuel,"* which is translated, *"God with us."*

Jesus fulfilled hundreds of Old Testament prophecies.
Here is a list of several such prophecies:
FULFILLED:

The Messiah would be the seed of a woman. Gen 3:15 Gal. 4:4

The Messiah would be a descendant of Abraham. Gen. 12:3 Matt. 1:1

The Messiah would be a descendant of Isaac. Gen. 17:19 Luke 3:34

The Messiah would be a descendant of Jacob. Num. 24:17 Matt. 1:2; 2:2

The Messiah would be from the tribe of Judah. Gen.49:10 Luke 3:33

The Messiah would be an heir to the throne of David. Is.9:7 Luke 1:32,33

The Messiah would be anointed and eternal. Ps.45:6,7; 102:25-27 Heb. 1:8-12

The Messiah would be born in Bethlehem.
Mic. 5:2 Luke 2:4,5,7

The Messiah would be born of a virgin. Is.7:14 Luke1:27,31

The Messiah's birth would trigger a slaughter of children. Jer.31:15 Matt.2:16-18

The Messiah would also come from Egypt. Hos.11:1 Matt.2:14,15

    The purpose of Jesus' birth and life was: He would save His people from their sins. What would He save us from? He would save us from eternal separation and damnation from our heavenly Father who created us in His image. A heavenly Father who is holy and cannot look at sin. A heavenly Father who loves us so much that He would send His only begotten Son to take our place and die for us on a cross.

John 3:16: For God so loved the world that He gave His only begotten Son, that whoever believes in Him should not perish but have everlasting life.

For God did not send His Son into the world to condemn the world, but that the world through Him might be saved. "He who believes in Him is not condemned; but he who does not believe is condemned already, because he has not believed in the name of the only begotten Son of God. And this is the condemnation, that the light has come into the world, and men loved darkness rather than light because their deeds were evil. For everyone practicing evil hates the light and does not come to the light, lest his deeds should be exposed. But he who does the truth comes to the light, that his deeds may be clearly seen, that they have been done in God."

The first step of salvation is believing in Jesus. Believing that He is the Son of God and believing that He died for our sins and arose again. ***Believing will get you to first base.*** But if you don't believe, the Bible says you are condemned already. And the condemnation is this, that men loving darkness rather than light. In other words we condemn ourselves when we choose the darkness rather than God's light.

God is a God of love. **1 John 4:8 says that God is love.** He loves us so much that <u>He gave His only begotten Son to take our place and die on the cross for our sins.</u> I don't know any other person who would have done that for me. His love is the purest, most complete love that we could ever know. No one loves you or I more than Jesus does!

God is also a holy God who cannot look at sin. Jesus's first message was to, **'Repent, for the kingdom of heaven is at hand.'** Repent means to not only be sorry for your sins, but to turn from your sins. It means to purpose in your heart that you will never do that again. You don't tell Jesus that you are sorry for your sins, and then keep sinning. Repent means to be sorry and to turn away from sin. **If we confess our sins, He is faithful and just to forgive us our sins and to cleanse us from all unrighteousness. 1 John 1:9**

Jesus began His ministry by calling fishermen and giving them a purpose. He told them to follow Him and He would make them fishers of men. In other words, He would give them a higher purpose. Instead of being consumed with fishing to provide food for their families, He would show them how to be consumed with fishing for men for the kingdom. ***A higher calling. A higher purpose.*** He wants to give each of us that purpose in life. A meaning for life; to save people from their sins.

In Matthew chapter 6, Jesus talks about worrying. Why do we worry? **Matt. 6:25-34 "Therefore I say to you, do not worry about your life, what you will eat or what you will drink; nor about your body, what you will put on. Is not life more than food and the body more than clothing? Look at the birds of the air, for they neither sow nor reap nor gather into barns; yet your heavenly Father feeds them. Are you not of more value than they?**

Which of you by worrying can add one cubit to his stature?

"So why do you worry about clothing? Consider the lilies of the field; how they grow: they neither toil nor spin; and yet I say to you that even Solomon in all his glory was not arrayed like one of these. Now if God so clothes the grass of the field, which today is, and tomorrow is thrown into the oven, will He not much more clothe you, O you of little faith?

"Therefore do not worry, saying, 'What shall we eat? Or 'What shall we drink?' or 'What shall we wear?' For after all these things the Gentiles seek. For your heavenly Father knows that you need all these things. <u>But seek first the kingdom of God and His righteousness, and all these things shall be added to you.</u> Therefore do not worry about tomorrow, for tomorrow will worry about its own things. Sufficient for the day is its own trouble".

This is one of my favorite scriptures, 'But seek first the kingdom of God and His righteousness, and all these things shall be added to you.' Notice it doesn't say might be added to you. These scriptures say it **shall be added to you.**

I held on to this verse going through the worst trial in my life. This verse kept bringing me back to what was most important. How can the Lord know that the birds need fed? How can He know how to beautify the flowers of the field? Because it is His Spirit in every living thing; from the tiniest insect to the largest mammal. From the cedars of Lebanon to the redwoods of California. From the lilies of the valley to the tulips of Holland. **It is His Spirit that gives 'LIFE' to the plants, animals and man, everything!**

Stay focused on Jesus. Follow Him. He will bring you through any circumstance!

Jesus then continues His ministry by healing the sick, casting out demons, opening blind eyes and deaf ears and brings the dead back to life. He shows many other wonderful miracles and signs, proving that He is the Messiah; the chosen one who would save His people from their sins.

Chapter 4 Bible Study:

1. What does the name *Immanuel* mean?

2. What was the purpose of Jesus' birth?

3. What was Jesus' first message?

4. What purpose did Jesus give the fishermen when He called them?

5. What does it mean to be 'Fishers of men'?

6. Jesus tells us not to worry, but to seek first these two things.

CHAPTER 5

THE KEYS OF THE KINGDOM

Having an understanding of who Jesus is, is the first step in obtaining the keys of the kingdom. Reading from **Matthew 16:13-20**

When Jesus came into the region of Caesarea Philippi, He asked His disciples, saying, "Who do Men say that I, the Son of Man, am?"

So, they said, "Some say John the Baptist, some Elijah, and others Jeremiah or one of the prophets."

He said to them, "But who do you say that I am?"

And Simon Peter answered and said, "You are the Christ, the Son of the living God."

Jesus answered and said to him, "Blessed are you Simon Bar-Jonah, for flesh and blood has not revealed this to you, but My Father who is in heaven.

And I also say to you that you are Peter, and on this rock I will build My church, and the gates of Hades shall not prevail against it.

And I will give you the keys of the kingdom of heaven, and whatever you bind on earth will be bound in heaven, and whatever you loose on earth will be loosed in heaven."

Then He commanded His disciples that they should tell no one that He was Jesus the Christ.

The word Christ means anointed One! The only begotten of the Father.

The One... the prophets spoke about centuries before;

the coming One, the Messiah,

the One who would save His people from their sins!

The One who would bruise Satan's head.

The One who would get the keys of death, hell and the grave.

The one who would defeat all the powers of darkness. _There is none greater._

There is no one else who would shed His blood on Calvary and take our sins upon Himself. The One who was obedient to the Father even to the point of death.

The One who loves us with an everlasting love.

The One who took our place on Calvary and died in our place so we could spend eternity with Him.

He deserves all the honor, power and glory!

When you really understand who Christ is, you are ready for the **Keys of the Kingdom.**

Keys can open doors or shut doors. They are essential for us to get into our houses, start our cars, open safes, unlock gates and many other things. Without our keys we would have trouble getting through a day.

Jesus told Peter that because he knew who He is, that he was blessed. Jesus then says that He will give him the Keys of the Kingdom of heaven, and whatever he binds on earth will be bound in heaven, and whatever he loose on earth will be loosed in heaven. These keys that Jesus is talking about will open doors or shut doors for us in the spiritual realm.

The first step in obtaining the keys is to be on the right side, to know Jesus. Once you make that commitment to accept Jesus in your heart, repent of sins and live your life for Him, you can have confidence in His leadership. He will give you the keys to bring kingdom living into your life.

So, before we can go into spiritual warfare, like any person getting ready to go into combat, preparations have to be made. We have to spend time in boot camp. We need to be on the right side and completely trust our commander-in-chief and what He requires of us. We have to be properly outfitted with our armor. We need to learn what our weapons are and how to use them. We have to understand who the enemy is, his tactics, his lies and his motives.

When you pass boot camp and are completely outfitted ……

you are ready for battle!

Chapter 5 Bible Study:

1. What is the first step in obtaining the Keys of the Kingdom?

2. What should we bind on earth?

3. What should we loosen on earth?

4. What does the word 'Christ' mean?

5. What four preparations we need to make before we can go into spiritual warfare?

CHAPTER 6

ARMOR OF GOD

As it says in **Ephesians 6:1-18**

Finally, my brethren, be strong in the Lord and in the power of His might. Put on the whole armor of God, that you may be able to stand against the wiles of the devil. For we do not wrestle against flesh and blood, but against principalities, against powers, against the rulers of the darkness of this age, against spiritual hosts of wickedness in the heavenly places. Therefore take up the whole armor of God, that you may be able to withstand in the evil day, and having done all, to stand. Stand therefore, having girded your waist with truth, having put on the breastplate of righteousness, and having shod your feet with the preparation of the gospel of peace; above all, taking the shield of faith with which you will be able to quench all the fiery darts of the wicked one. And take the helmet of salvation, and the sword of the Spirit, which is the word of God; praying always with all prayer

and supplication in the Spirit, being watchful to this end with all perseverance and supplication for all the saints.

We are instructed to put on the **whole armor** of God, because it could be possible that we only put on some of the armor. Each piece of armor has a purpose for our protection. Leaving some of the armor off would open us up to injury and/or attack from Satan. When a soldier girds himself to fight in a battle, his whole body needs protection.

Lets take a look at the different pieces of armor that we need, and how they protect us from the evil one.

Chapter 6 Bible Study:

1. What will protect us to stand against the wiles of the devil?

2. True of False: We wrestle against flesh and blood.

3. What piece of armor will quench all the fiery darts of the wicked one?

4. What piece of armor will protect our thoughts?

CHAPTER 7

PUTTING ON THE HELMET OF SALVATION

Once you decide that you want to be on the right side, Jesus' command is to repent and believe the gospel. In **John 3:1-21** There is a religious man that comes to Jesus by night. His name is Nicodemus. In verse 3: **Jesus answered and said to him, "Most assuredly, I say to you, unless one is born again he cannot see the kingdom of God."** Nicodemus questions how this can be. He asks can he enter a second time into his mother's womb and be born? Jesus answered, **"Most assuredly, I say to you, unless one is born of water and the Spirit, he cannot enter the kingdom of God. That which is born of the flesh is flesh, and that which is born of the Spirit is spirit."**

Being born of the Spirit means breaking before the Lord in total repentance and asking Jesus to forgive you of all sin and unrighteousness.

It is a surrendering of self and acknowledging Jesus as Lord. It is a matter of your heart. True repentance is not just speaking out words, but a **total** breaking of your heart. You will know when you are born of the Spirit for Jesus' Spirit will come into your spirit and you will feel a new awakening. Everything will be clear and fresh and new, just like a newborn baby. It's not a guessing game. You will know without a doubt that you are born again **when you truly repent** and His Spirit witnesses with your spirit.

The second step is being baptized by **immersion** once you have committed to follow Jesus. Jesus began His ministry by being baptized Himself in the Jordon River by John the Baptist. Jesus led by example. Being baptized represents dying to the old man; washing your sins away and rising to the new man in Christ. It is a baptism of repentance. Jesus said in **Mark 1:14 "The time is fulfilled, and the kingdom of God is at hand. Repent, and believe the gospel."** To be baptized, you have to be old enough to repent. Some churches baptize babies, but a child before he comes to the age of accountability is already saved.

Repentance is from the heart. You have to be sincerely sorry for your sins and make that commitment to follow Jesus. Many people get saved the moment they repent of sins and make that commitment to follow Jesus, and afterwards are baptized. Some get saved the day they are baptized. Remember it is not the baptism that saves you...it is your heart!

The steps of salvation are:

1. **Believe that Jesus died for you.**

2. **Confess Him as your Lord and Savior.**

3. **Repent, be sorry and turn from sin.**

Romans 10:9,10 Says this, "That if you confess with your mouth the Lord Jesus and believe in your heart that God has raised Him from the dead, you will be saved.

For with the heart one believes to righteousness, and with the mouth confession is made to salvation."

Romans 3:10 There is none righteous, no, not one;

Romans 3:23 For all have sinned and fall short of the glory of God.

If you have made that commitment to follow Jesus, you now have the right to put your helmet of salvation on. Congratulations! You have made a wise decision.

    A helmet is a piece of armor that protects our head. Since we are in a spiritual battle the helmet protects us from all the negative thoughts the enemy throws at us. Remember the battle ground starts in our thoughts processes, the mind. We must be keen in the spirit and realize that the enemy of our souls is the accuser of the brethren and we must resist him with speaking out the Word of God, the Sword of the Spirit.

The enemy aka Satan and his demons, are constantly working, scheming and setting traps for us. Satan will use our closest friends, relatives and acquaintances to trip us up. Always keep this in mind. We do not wrestle against flesh and blood, but against principalities, against powers, against the rulers of darkness, against spiritual wickedness in the heavenly places. So, if someone says something degrading to you or derogatory and it hits your spirit like a lead spike, you can be certain it wasn't from the Lord. For the Lord is kind, patience and loving. He always sees the best in us. He always has our best interests in mind.

The fruit of the Spirit is love, joy, peace, long suffering, kindness, goodness, faithfulness, gentleness, self-control. The Bible tells us to test the Spirit. If someone is acting contrary to the fruit of the Spirit you can be sure it is from the enemy. Put on your helmet and resist him in the name of the Lord!

Chapter 7 Bible Study:

1. What does Jesus say that one must do to see the kingdom of Heaven?

2. What did Jesus do before He started His ministry?

3. To be baptized, you must be old enough to _____.

4. True or False: A child before he comes to an age of accountability is already saved.

5. True or False: There is none righteous, no, not one.

6. Name four of the fruits of the Spirit.

CHAPTER 8

PUTTING ON THE BELT OF TRUTH

In Ephesians chapter 6, the Bible says to gird our waist with truth. Some translations say to put on the belt of truth. If we are instructed to put on the belt of truth or gird our waist with truth then I guess it could be fair to say that we can forget to put on the belt of truth, or not put the belt of truth on. So, what is the belt of truth?

Looking into God's word, we read in John 14:6 that Jesus says, **"I am the way, the truth and the life. No one comes to the Father except through Me."** Here we find that Jesus is the way to the Father, He is the life and He is the truth. So Jesus is truth. What else does the Bible say about Jesus?

In **John chapter 1:1-5 In the beginning was the Word, and the Word was with God, and the Word was God. He was in the beginning with God. All things were made through Him, and**

without Him nothing was made that was made. In Him was life, and the life was the light of men. And the light shines in the darkness, and the darkness did not comprehend it. And reading from verse **14: And the Word became flesh and dwelt among us, and we beheld His glory, the glory as of the only begotten of the Father, full of grace and truth.** So here we have it:

WORD=GOD=LIFE=LIGHT=JESUS =TRUTH

So therefore if Jesus says He is the truth and Jesus is the Word of God that came in the flesh, we have to conclude then that truth is the Word of God.

So putting on the belt of truth, means to read your Word, the Bible. Be filled up with the Word of God so no enemy can trick you or mislead you.

The psalmist said in Psalms **119:11 Your word I have hidden in my heart, that I might not sin against You.** Jesus also says in **John 15:7 "If you abide in Me, and My words abides in you, you will ask what you desire, and it shall be done for you".**

Chapter 8 Bible Study:

1. Who said, 'I am the way, the truth and the life.'

2. Yes or No: If we are instructed to put on the belt of truth, could it be possible to not put it on?

3. All things were made through whom?

4. What do we have to abide in so our desires would be done for us?

CHAPTER 9

BREASTPLATE OF RIGHTEOUSNESS

In Ephesians we are instructed to put on the breastplate of righteousness, therefore we can conclude that it is possible to not put it on. Why does the Bible say breastplate? When a soldier gets suited up for battle, one of his pieces of armor is the breastplate. The breastplate covers a soldier's heart. Putting on a breastplate of righteousness means to be determine to guard your heart, to walk uprightly before the Lord, obeying His commands and giving no place to the enemy. The Lord is a God of righteousness. He is a holy God and He expects His people to be a holy people.

2 Corinthians 6:14-18 Do not be *unequally yoked together with unbelievers.* For what fellowship has righteousness with lawlessness? And what communion has light with darkness? And what accord has Christ with Beliel? Or what part has a believer with an unbeliever?

And what agreement has the temple of God with idols? For you are the temple of the living God. As God has said: "I will dwell in them and walk among them. I will be their God, and they shall be My people." Therefore "Come out from among them and be separate, says the Lord. Do not touch what is unclean, and I will receive you." "I will be a Father to you, and you shall be My sons and daughters, says the Lord Almighty."

In **Matthew chapter 7:13:** Jesus also admonishes us, **"Enter by the narrow gate; for wide is the gate and broad is the way that leads to destruction, and there are many who go in by it. Because narrow is the gate and difficult is the way which leads to life, and there are few who find it."**

Walk rightly before the Lord. Everyday when you rise, make a declaration to the Lord by saying, '***This day I am going to follow You.*** I am going to walk in your ways giving no place to the devil, knowing that God is light and in Him is no darkness at all.'

Chapter 9 Bible Study:

1. Putting on the breastplate of righteousness will guard a soldier's_____.

2. What does the word 'righteousness' mean?

3. 2Cor 6:14-18 says not to be unequally yoked together with unbelievers. What does that mean?

4. We are the temple of who?

CHAPTER 10

SHOD YOUR FEET WITH THE PREPARATION OF THE GOSPEL OF PEACE

I have horses, and every so often, I have to put new shoes on their feet. They need to be shod so I can ride them without their feet getting sore and tender. When their feet are properly shod our ride is smooth and pleasant. We can go for miles on a new set of shoes.

The Bible instructs us to shod our feet with the preparation of the gospel of peace. For us to go out with the gospel, we must be prepared. We have to have God's word in our hearts, be prayed up, be in tune with the Holy Spirit and then go with it! **Go out and preach the gospel.** That is the great commission. For what good is it to have God's word in our hearts if we sit at home and never tell anyone the good news?

In **Matt 28:18** And Jesus came and spoke to them saying, "All authority has been given to me in heaven and on earth. Go therefore and make disciples of all the nations, baptizing them in the name of the Father and of the Son and of the Holy Spirit, teaching them to observe all things that I have commanded you; and lo, I am with you always, even to the end of the age." Amen.

Reading your Bible daily is the key for victory in your life.

Jesus said in **John chapter 15: "I am the true vine, and My Father is the vinedresser. Every branch in Me that does not bear fruit He takes away; and every branch that bears fruit He prunes, that it may bear more fruit.**

You are already clean because of the word which I have spoken to you.

Abide in Me, and I in you. As the branch cannot bear fruit of itself, unless it abides in the vine, neither can you, unless you abide in Me.

I am the vine, you are the branches. He who abides in Me, and I in him, bears much fruit; for without Me you can do nothing.

If anyone does not abide in Me, he is cast out as a branch and is withered; and they gather them and throw them into the fire, and they are burned.

If you abide in Me, and My words abide in you, you will ask what you desire, and it shall be done for you.

By this My Father is glorified, that you bear much fruit; so you will be My disciples."

As you read your Bible, you are abiding in Jesus, for Jesus is the Word of God.

John 1:14 And the Word became flesh and dwelt among us, and we beheld His glory, the glory as of the only begotten of the Father, full of grace and truth.

So, the great promise in all of this is, as you read your Bible, you are abiding in Jesus. As *you abide in Jesus, you can ask whatever you desire and* the Lord will do it. *Now that's a great promise!*

Some people have told me that when they try to read the Bible, they don't understand it. I always advise them to pray before they read. Ask the Lord to open up their understanding and enlighten them concerning His Word. You will be amazed how the Lord will make His Word come to life and leap off the pages. He wants you to know His Word. Remember to ask, seek and knock. He will not withhold any good gift from you.

Chapter 10 Bible Study:

1. Why does the scripture say to shod your feet?

2. What does the preparation of the gospel mean?

3. What two things must new disciples do?

4. What promise do we have if we abide in God's word?

CHAPTER 11

TAKING UP THE SHIELD OF FAITH

Faith, what is it? We can't see it, we can't hold it...so what is it? **Hebrews 11:1 says, Now faith is the substance of things hoped for, the evidence of things not seen.** The substance of things hoped for. Faith is hoping in something. It is believing that something will happen. It is an intangible belief in something or someone.

Hebrews 11:3 By faith we understand that the worlds were framed by the word of God, so that the things which are seen were not made of things which are visible. Reading on in Hebrews for some examples of faith by our patriarchs verse **4-6: By faith Abel offered to God a more excellent sacrifice than Cain, through which he obtained witness that he was righteous, God testifying of his gifts; and through it he being dead still speaks.**

By faith Enoch was taken away so that he did not see death, "and was not found, because God had taken him"; for before he was taken he had this testimony, that he pleased God. But without faith it is impossible to please Him, for he who comes to God must believe that He is, and that He is a rewarder of those who diligently seek Him.

Having faith is the core of our walk with God. Faith is what pleases the Lord. And knowing that the Lord will reward us, gives us that needed incentive to keep going on. One of my greatest answers to prayer was during a trying time in my marriage. I wrote about this in my book, 'A Preacher Girl's Ride of Faith.' I will summarize it here.

Butch and I were married twelve years and were busy with our jobs and working around the house, when out of the blue…Butch left me. I was devastated. I felt like my whole world came crashing down. Depression set in. How would I ever make it? Could I keep the farm running on my income alone? It was during this time that Jesus started dealing with me. He asked me if I would give up everything and follow Him?

I had already lost my identical twin sister to cancer and at this time in my life, my husband left me. So I said to Jesus, "Lord, I lost Debbie and now Butch, what do you want me to do? I will do whatever you want". I committed my life to Jesus that day. I started praying and reading my Bible. I attended every church service. Everyone told me to give up and throw the towel in, our marriage was over. I told them, "No I was not giving up!" My Bible says that nothing is impossible for the Lord. After being gone almost a year with no hope in sight, things started getting worse. I was losing my full time job and finances were getting low. I took a horse to a sale in Scottdale, Pa. but I could not sell the horse. Driving home ten o'clock that night, I pulled in the driveway, led the horse out of the trailer and as I was walking behind the back of my house, I looked up to heaven. All the stars were out. The night sky looked so serene and peaceful. Gazing up to heaven I said to Jesus, "Lord, I don't know what else to do. I just want to remind you, Butch isn't home. I'm losing my full time job and I couldn't make a sell with this horse. But I am not giving up! I still got faith in you!

As I led the horse through the corral area, my name was called out. I heard 'Barb.' I thought 'did I just hear my name?' I put the horse in its stall, fed it some grain and hay and walking out of the barn I heard my name called again. It was 10:30 at night and there was just me and the horse, and the horse was not Mr. Ed, he couldn't speak. I said to the Lord, "Lord this must be you, but I don't know what else you want me to do. I'm at every prayer meeting, going to church service and reading my Bible. So I am going to go in the house and go to bed." The next morning Butch was home!
The miracle happened! Speaking out my faith in the midst of my trials, moved the hand of God. There is nothing more powerful in the spirit realm than your faith. **And speaking out your faith becomes your Sword of the Spirit.** We will cover that later in more detail.

Notice that the Lord does not give us any armor for our backs. That is because we are to confront our enemy head on. Now that we have our armor on, it's time to take up our weapons.

Chapter 11 Bible Study:

1. What is faith?

2. Yes or No: Is it possible to please God without faith?

3. What will the shield of faith stop?

4. What two things must a person believe who comes to God?

CHAPTER 12

Weapons of Warfare
2 Corinthians 10:3-6

For though we walk in the flesh, we do not war according to the flesh. For the weapons of our warfare are not carnal but mighty in God for pulling down strong holds, casting down arguments and every high thing that exalts itself against the knowledge of God, bringing every thought into captivity to the obedience of Christ, and being ready to punish all disobedience when your obedience is fulfilled.

This passage of scripture tells us:

1. We are in a war
2. We have weapons
3. Our weapons are not in this realm. They are not carnal. **They are spiritual weapons.**
4. They are mighty weapons in God.
5. They will pull down strongholds.
6. They will cast down arguments and every high thing that exalts itself against the knowledge of God.
7. They will bring every thought into captivity to the obedience of Christ.
8. They will punish all disobedience when our obedience is fulfilled.

What exactly are our SPIRITUAL WEAPONS

1. **TOTAL SUBMISSION:** LOVE and OBEDIENCE
2. **PRAYER AND FASTING**
3. **BAPTISM OF THE HOLY SPIRIT**…. All prayer and supplication in the spirit.
4. **PRAISE**…………….Pushes back the darkness.
5. **THE SPOKEN WORD OF GOD IS …. THE SWORD OF THE SPIRIT!**

    A. The Word of God

    B. The Name of Jesus

    C. The Blood of Jesus

    D. Binding and Loosing

6. **ENGAGING THE BATTLE….FAITH**

7. **FERVENCY** --------means hot, burning, glowing. Having or showing great warmth of feeling: intensely earnest. Fervent means to boil, glow, hot, burning.

Chapter 12 Bible Study:

1. If our weapons of warfare are not carnal, what kind of weapons are they?

2. Name four things that our weapons are capable of doing?

3. Name our seven Spiritual Weapons.

Chapter 13

TOTAL SUBMISSION

James 4:7 says, Therefore submit to God. Resist the devil and he will flee from you. Draw near to God and He will draw near to you. Cleanse your hands, you sinners; and purify your hearts, you doubleminded. Lament and mourn and weep! Let your laughter be turned to mourning and your joy to gloom. Humble yourselves in the sight of the Lord, and He will lift you up.

The more you submit to God, the more powerful you are in the spirit realm. The more you read your Bible, walk in righteousness, speak the truth, obey the commandments, the more powerful you are. Satan no longer sees 'you' but he sees the Lord Jesus Christ in you, as it says in **Romans 13:14 But put on the Lord Jesus Christ, and make no provision for the flesh, to fulfill its lusts.**

1Peter 2:13-15: Therefore submit yourselves to every ordinance of man for the Lord's sake

whether to the king as supreme, or to governors, as to those who are sent by him for the punishment of evildoers and for the praise of those who do good. For this is the will of God, that by doing good you may put to silence the ignorance of foolish men--The Lord has put all law and government in place. By obeying the law of the land, we are obeying the Lord.

Also in **1Peter 5:6-9 Therefore humble yourselves under the mighty hand of God, that He may exalt you in due time, casting all your care upon Him, for He cares for you. Be sober, be vigilant; because your adversary the devil walks about like a roaring lion, seeking whom he may devour. Resist him, steadfast in the faith, knowing that the same sufferings are experienced by your brotherhood in the world.** The more we submit and humble ourselves, the more the Lord will exalt us in due time. We all have a due time if we will listen and obey the Lord.

LOVE

I cherish the scriptures on love in

1 Corinthians chapter 13: I-13 I believe these scriptures should be posted in every house, every building and every business. Beginning at verse 1:

Though I speak with the tongues of men and of angels, but have not love, I have become as sounding brass or a clanging cymbal. And though I have the gift of prophecy, and understand all mysteries and all knowledge, and though I have all faith, so that I could remove mountains, but have not love, I am nothing. And though I bestow all my goods to feed the poor, and though I give my body to be burned, but have not love, it profits me nothing.

Love suffers long and is kind; love does not envy; love does not parade itself, is not puffed up; does not behave rudely, does not seek its own, is not provoked, thinks no evil; does not rejoice in iniquity, but rejoices in the truth; bears all things, believes all things, hopes all things, endures all things.

Love never fails. But whether there are prophecies, they will fail; whether there are tongues, they will cease; whether there is knowledge, it will vanish away. For we know in part and we prophesy in part. But when that which is perfect has come, then that which is in part will be done away.

When I was a child, I spoke as a child, I understood as a child, I thought as a child; but when I became a man, I put away childish things.

For now we see in a mirror, dimly, but then face to face. Now I know in part, but then I shall know just as I also am known.

And now abide faith, hope, love, these three; *but the greatest of these is love.*

Jesus says in John chapter 14 that He gives us a new commandment; that we love one another; as He has loved us. He says that by this all will know that we are His disciples, if we have love one for another.

The Bible says that God is love. Isn't it great to know that our heavenly Father is a God of love.

This love flows from His throne to us. A Christian should always be showing love. **John 3:16 For God so loved the world that He gave His only begotten Son, that whoever believeth should not perish, but have everlasting life.** If you are around someone who says they are a Christian, but you don't see the love, I would question their salvation.

OBEDIENCE

Everyone wants the blessings in this life. We want the perfect relationship, the best paying job, the coolest friends, the fastest car etc. But a lot of people are not willing to pay the price. Having the blessings of life comes with a price tag. There is a price that must be paid. Each blessing has a price tag on it that says: obedience. And each act of obedience is lined with a sacrifice. Just like Jesus when he died on the cross for our sins; he paid the price and laid down His life as a living sacrifice. Because of His obedience God the Father has highly exalted Him.

Philippians 2: 5-11 says: Let this mind be in you which was also in Christ Jesus, who, being in

the form of God, did not consider it robbery to be equal with God, but made Himself of no reputation, taking the form of a servant, and coming in the likeness of men. And being found in appearance a man, He humbled himself and became obedient to the point of death, even the death of the cross. Therefore God also has highly exalted him and given Him the name which is above every name, that at the name of Jesus every knee should bow, of those in heaven, and of those on earth, and of those under the earth, and that every tongue should confess that Jesus Christ is Lord, to the glory of God the Father.

In Deuteronomy chapter 11:26-28 The Lord says, "Behold, I set before you today a blessing and a curse: the blessing, if you obey the commandments of the Lord your God which I command you today; and a curse, if you do not obey the commandments of the Lord your God, but turn aside from the way which I command you today, to go after other gods which you have not known."

I have often preached, *'In the obedience the Lord commands the blessings.'*

If we truly love the Lord, we will obey Him. Jesus also says in John **14:15 "If you love Me, keep My commandments."** He also says in verse 21,23,24, **"He who has My commandments and keeps them, it is he who loves Me. And He who loves Me will be loved by My Father, and I will love him and manifest Myself to him." "If anyone loves Me, he will keep My word; and My Father will love him, and We will come to him and make Our home with him. He who does not love Me does not keep My words; and the word which you hear is not Mine but the Father's who sent Me."**

The Lord knows how much we love Him, by how much we obey Him. Always remember it is the Lord who blesses. The more obedient you are, the more you will be blessed! You don't have to make it happen, the Lord will command it!

In the obedience the Lord commands the blessings!

Chapter 13 Bible Study:

1. What two things must you do for the devil to flee from you?

2. True or False: The more you submit to God, the more powerful you become in the spirit realm.

3. Yes or No: It is the will of God that we submit to every ordinance of man.

4. Because the devil walks about like a roaring lion, seeking whom he may devour, what three things should we be doing?

5. What two attributes do you need to be submitted?

6. How will all men know we are Jesus' disciples?

7. In the obedience the Lord commands the _____.

Chapter 14

PRAYER AND FASTING

Prayer is our intimate communion with our heavenly Father. Many new believers starting out will often question, 'How do you pray?' 'Is there a right way?' 'Am I praying correctly?' These same questions were ask in biblical times, so Jesus addresses this issue.

In **Matthew 6:5-15 "And when you pray, you shall not be like the hypocrites. For they love to pray standing in the synagogues and on the corners of the streets, that they may be seen by men. Assuredly, I say to you, they have their reward. But you, when you pray, go into your room, and when you have shut your door, pray to your Father who is in the *secret place*; and your Father who sees in secret will reward you openly. And when you pray, do not use vain repetitions as the heathen do. For they think that they will be heard for their many words.**

Therefore do not be like them. For your Father knows the things you have need of before you ask Him.

In this manner, therefore, pray:

> Our Father in heaven,
>
> Hallowed be Your name.
>
> Your kingdom come.
>
> Your will be done
>
> On earth as it is in heaven.
>
> Give us this day our daily bread.
>
> And forgive us our debts,
>
> As we forgive our debtors.
>
> And do not lead us into temptation,
>
> But deliver us from the evil one.
>
> For Yours is the kingdom and the
>
> power and the glory forever. Amen."

"For if you forgive men their trespasses, your heavenly Father will also forgive you. But if you do not forgive men their trespasses, neither will your Father forgive your trespasses."

You might say, 'I can say that prayer in 10 seconds, so how can I spend intimate time with the Lord?' Well, break the prayer down and spend 10 minutes on each sentence.

For example: Spend time praising and worshiping the Lord on the first sentence.

On the second sentence: Ask that His will be done in the world, your nation, your government, your family, friends, neighbors then yourself. Spending time on each subject.

On the third sentence ask for anything that you have need of, also mention your plans, dreams and goals. Talk to Him like your best friend.

On the fourth sentence, let the Lord examine your heart and confess any short comings, trespasses or sins. Also make sure you are not holding anything against another. You don't want any bitterness to take root in your spirit.

On the last sentence, ask for God's protection over yourself, family and friends.

This is where you can use spiritual warfare. Before you know it, you would have spent quality time with the Lord.

Now if you want to bump your prayers up a notch, include fasting. Why is fasting important? What significance can that have?

When you fast, you are denying the body of something that it needs...food. If you are denying the body then you are making a sacrifice. When you are making a sacrifice, you are showing how determined you are to get an answer to your prayers.

Jesus said in **Matthew 6:16-18 "More over, when you fast, do not be like the hypocrites, with a sad countenance. For they disfigure their faces that they many appear to men to be fasting. Assuredly, I say to you, they have their reward. But you, when you fast, anoint your head and wash your face, so that you do not appear to men to be fasting, but to your Father who is in the secret place; and your Father who sees in secret will reward you openly."**

In the book of Daniel, we find Daniel fasting and praying twenty-one days. An angel appears to him and tells him that on the first day of his supplication, his prayers were heard, and he had come because of his words. The angel goes on and tells Daniel that a prince of Persia withstood him twenty-one days. This prince is a demonic angel sent to stop his prayer requests. So, don't give up praying, keep your faith. Pray until the answer comes through.

When Jesus was questioned by his disciples why they could not cast out a demon in a young boy, and He could, Jesus responded. **"Because of your unbelief; for assuredly, I say to you, if you have faith as a mustard seed, you will say to this mountain, 'Move from here to there,' and it will move; and nothing will be impossible for you. However, this kind does not go out except by prayer and fasting."**

So fasting puts some muscle behind your prayers. It moves the hand of God. No demon of hell can withstand a person so committed.

Jesus said in **Matthew 7:7-12 "Ask, and it will be given to you; seek, and you will find, knock, and it will be opened to you. For everyone who asks receives, and he who seeks finds, and to him who knocks it will be opened. Or what man is there among you who, if his son asks for bread, will give him a stone? Or if he asks for a fish, will he give him a serpent? If you then, being evil, know how to give good gifts to your children, how much more will your Father who is in heaven give good things to those who ask Him! Therefore whatever you want men to do to you, do also to them, for this is the law and the Prophets"**.

Remember you have not because you ask not! Ask and you shall receive! Asking requires putting your faith into action. You have to believe that the Lord can do it. You have to believe that He is concerned about everything you are concerned with, from the biggest to the tiniest. He is the God of the universe! Nothing is too hard for Him.

Prayer is our intimate communication line to the Lord. It is a line that doesn't get a busy signal. It is a line that isn't put on hold for another call. It is a line that won't be disconnected.

The Lord is near to us, as near as our very own lips, all we have to do is speak, and He hears us! The God who sits on the throne in heaven is as close to you as your very own lips! Why is that? How can that be? Because the Spirit that created the whole world and everything that is in it, is the same Spirit that is in you!

Jesus said in **Matthew 10:29 "Are not two sparrows sold for a copper coin? And not one of them falls to the ground apart from your Father's will. But the very hairs of your head are all numbered. Do not fear therefore; you are of more value than many sparrows."**

How can God know when a sparrow falls to the ground? Because God's Spirit that created everything and everybody, also created that sparrow. The sparrow is living only because it has the spirit of the living God in it. So, when that sparrow dies, its spirit returns to the Father. The same way with us, when we die our Spirit will return to the Father and our relationship to the Lord will be measured on the scales. Did we know Jesus? Did we follow Him? Did we do the will of the Father?

Chapter 14 Bible Study:

1. True or False: We are not to use vain repetitions when we pray.

2. True or False: Once we greet the Father in our prayer, the first thing we should do is praise Him.

3. Why is fasting important?

4. How many days did Daniel pray before his answer came through?

5. What does the 'secret place' mean?

CHAPTER 15

Baptism of the Holy Spirit

I love the story about John the Baptist. He was the predecessor for Jesus. The one who would prepare the way. **Matt 3:3 For this is he who was spoken of by the prophet Isaiah, saying: "The voice of one crying in the wilderness; 'Prepare the way of the Lord; Make His paths straight.' "** He was a rough, tough preacher man who didn't hold back, but told people exactly how it was. His first message was "Repent, for the kingdom of heaven is at hand!" You can read about him in Matthew chapter 3.

Years ago I was planning on doing a water baptism for over twenty people in my ministry. As I was seeking the Lord and praying, I asked the Lord if He would give me something very hot from His throne, something that no one had ever heard before. Another preacher was coming to help me with the baptism for I didn't have my credentials yet. So, I prayed for the Lord to give me something 'very hot' so this preacher would believe that He had called me.

Not that I needed his approval for I already had the Lord's, but just to confirm to him my calling.

When I pray, I always ask questions. So, this day I asked the Lord, "Why did John the Baptist wear camel hair? He could have worn bear hide, rabbit fur, fox or any other hide or fur, but why camel?" Immediately the Holy Spirit asked me, "What does a camel do?" I answered and said, "It carries burdens for people." "So who was John the Baptist pointing to the Holy Spirit asked" I answered, "Jesus, the one who would carry our burdens."

So now I asked, "Why did he eat honey and locusts? He could have eaten grasshoppers and crickets. But why honey and locusts? Again, the Holy Spirit told me to check it out in His Word. In **Psalm 119:103 How sweet are Your words to my taste, Sweeter than honey to my mouth!** So, honey represents eating the word of God. Makes sense since he is a preacher, he would be reading and preaching God's word. But what could eating locusts represent? The Lord again said to check it out in His word. In the old testament, locusts were always sent to destroy the green herb, grass etc.

They were always sent as a plague. Now the Lord said, put it together. **"Eat my word and you can eat the destroyer! Don't eat my word and the destroyer can eat you!" Wow!** What a revelation! I never heard it preached before. It pays to ask questions.

I was now curious about everything concerning John the Baptist. So I continued to ask another question. This time I asked, "Why did John the Baptist wear a leather belt around his waist?" The Lord asked me, "If you see a person coming toward you with a leather belt, what would you think?" I answered and said, "I would think I was in a lot of trouble!" "You answered correctly." The leather belt represents the one who would have all authority in heaven and on earth....Jesus!

It's also important to note that Isaiah said John the Baptist was, 'The voice of one crying in the wilderness.' That means that if John the Baptist could be the voice of one and make such a huge difference, so can we. We can all be the voice of one. We can all make a difference. We all need to start crying in the wilderness (darkness).

John then gives us our first mention of the Holy Spirit. In verse 3:11 **"I indeed baptize you with water unto repentance, but He who is coming after me is mightier than I, whose sandals I am not worthy to carry. He will baptize you with the Holy Spirit and fire"**. Not only does John mentioned the Holy Spirit but he mentions a word that is very significant, 'fire'. The purpose of the Holy Spirit is to put us on 'fire' for the Lord.

Jesus talks about the Holy Spirit in **John 14:15-18 "If you love Me, keep my commandments. And I will pray the Father, and He will give you another Helper, that He may abide with you forever---the Spirit of truth, whom the world cannot receive, because it neither sees Him nor knows Him; but you know Him, for He dwells with you and will be in you. I will not leave you orphans; I will come to you."** Again, the Holy Spirit is mention in verse **25-27 "These things I have spoken to you while being present with you. But the Helper, the Holy Spirit, whom the Father will send in My name, He will teach you all things, and bring to your remembrance all things that I said to you.**

Peace I leave with you, My peace I give to you; not as the world gives do I give to you. Let not your heart be troubled, neither let it be afraid."

The Holy Spirit is referred to as the Helper, the Spirit of truth, the teacher and peace. There is nothing in this realm that can comfort us and give us that peace we all are seeking. It is worth more than all the riches in the world. Money can't buy that assurance.

The next place the Holy Spirit is mentioned in the Bible is **Acts 1:4-5**. Jesus commands the disciples not to depart from Jerusalem, but to wait for the promise of the Father. He said, **"You have heard from Me, for John truly baptized with water, but you shall be baptized with the Holy Spirit not many days from now."** In verse 8: Jesus mentions that they shall receive power when the Holy Spirit has come upon them, and then they shall be witnesses to Jesus in Jerusalem and all the world. So, the Holy Spirit is a promise from the Father. It is to equip us for ministry. It is to anoint us with power and fire. Jesus is the baptizer of the Holy Spirit.

He wants all believers to be baptized so we can be the best witnesses for Him and the kingdom.

So how do you get this baptism? First you have to believe in it and then believe that it is for you. Then you have to ask Jesus for it, since He is the baptizer. Then wait for the promise. It might not happen the first time you pray for it or the second or third, but don't give up. Be like the persistent widow. Keep asking, keep seeking until you get it. Jesus wants to baptize you!

Chapter 15 Bible Study:

1. What was John the Baptist's first message?

2. Why did John the Baptist wear camel's hair?

3. What does eating honey and locusts mean?

4. Who did John the Baptist say would baptize us with the Holy Spirit?

5. Name four titles given to the Holy Spirit.

6. What would the disciples receive after getting the Holy Spirit?

CHAPTER 16

PRAISE
A WEAPON THAT PUSHES BACK THE DARKNESS

There are many scriptures in the Bible about praise. Here are a few that I noted.

Psalm 50:23 Whoever offers praise glorifies Me; and to him who orders his conduct aright I will show the salvation of God.

Psalm 145:3 Great is the Lord, and greatly to be praised; and His greatness is unsearchable.

Psalm 149:6,7 Let the high praises of God be in their mouths, and a two-edged sword in their hand.

Psalm 150:6 Let everything that has breath praise the Lord.

Psalm 22:3 But You are holy, Who inhabits the praises of Israel.

Psalm 100:4 Enter into His gates with thanks giving, and into His courts with praise.

When we praise the Lord, we glorify Him. That means we are honoring Him. Recognizing Him as the great King, God Almighty. We are exalting His name above all others and bringing glory and honor to Him.

When we do this, we get His attention. It pleases Him to hear His creation honoring Him. It lifts His Spirit. It brings His presence into our situation. He inhabits our praises. He shows up. The same feeling of gratitude, love, and happiness that we get when someone pays us a compliment or recognizes our achievements is the same feeling that the Lord feels when we praise Him.

Praise pushes back the darkness. Satan can't stand it when we praise the Lord because he wanted to be God. He wanted to receive all the recognition and honor. He started out being the Praise and Worship leader in heaven until his pride was lifted up. When he hears praise going up he takes off. Praise pushes him back!

In Genesis chapter 29, we read the story of Jacob; son of Israel, when he marries Leah and Rachel. The Bible says that Leah's eyes were delicate, but Rachel was beautiful of form and appearance. It also says that Jacob loved Rachel and Leah was unloved. When the Lord saw that Leah was unloved, He opened her womb; but Rachel was barren.

Leah goes on and conceived four sons to Jacob. The first she names Reuben; for she said, **"The Lord has surely looked on my affliction. Now therefore, my husband will love me."** The second she named Simeon and said, **"Because the Lord has heard that I am unloved, He has therefore given me this son also."** The third son she named Levi; and said, **"Now this time my husband will become attached to me, because I have borne him three sons."** And the fourth son, she named Judah, and said, **"Now I will praise the Lord."** She later would conceive and bear two more sons and a daughter.

The children of Jacob would become the twelve tribes of Israel. The tribe that would be in charge of praise and worship was Judah.

In the book of Judges, chapter 1:1-19 the children of Israel asked the Lord, saying, **"Who shall be first to go up for us against the Canaanites to fight against them?"** And the Lord said, **"Judah shall go up, Indeed I have delivered the land into his hand."** Judah was always sent first in battle. They would sing and praise the Lord ahead of the rest of the tribes. *Praise always pushes back the darkness.* When Judah went first the battle was won. What does that mean to us? No matter what circumstance we find ourselves in, no matter what we are facing, always praise the Lord first, and watch how He will win the battle for you. During the reign of David, over 4000 musicians were assigned to sing in the temple night and day.

1Chronicles 9:33, 23:5. Why were they assigned? Because praise brings the presence of the Lord into the temple. It brings the presence of the Lord into our situation.

When we look at a story in the New Testament, **Acts 16:16-34**, Paul and Silas rebuked a spirit to come out of a girl, that brought her masters much profit. They were seized, beaten and thrown into prison.

The jailer was commanded to keep them securely. **Having received such a charge he put them into the inner prison and fastened their feet in the stocks. But at mid-night, Paul and Silas were praying and singing hymns to God, and the prisoners were listening to them. Suddenly there was a great earth quake so that the foundations of the prison were shaken; and immediately all the doors were opened and everyone's chains were loosed.**

Praise will shake the foundation of your prison and loosen your chains. What bondage or addiction is keeping you captive? Is it drugs, alcohol, sexual perversion, greed, lust, pornography, food etc. Start praising the Lord. Praise will open the doors of freedom for you and set you free! Give it a try.

Chapter 16 Bible Study:

1. What weapon pushes back the darkness?

2. What does Judah mean?

3. What tribe would always go first in battle?

4. What does praise bring into our situation?

5. If you want to shake the foundations of your prison, what should you do?

CHAPTER 17

SPEAKING INTO YOUR DARKNESS

If you are sick and tired of the enemy robbing you of your relationships, your finances, your peace, your happiness and your health, and want to see breakthroughs in your life then it's time to engage the battle. Know this, Jesus always wins.

Reading from Genesis 1:1-5

In the beginning God created the heavens and the earth.

The earth was without form, and void; and darkness was on the face of the deep. And the spirit of God was hovering over the face of the waters.

Then God said, "Let there be light"; and there was light.

And God saw the light, that it was good; and God divided the light from the darkness.

God called the light Day, and the darkness He called Night. So the evening and the morning were the first day.

Take note that the earth had no form and was void, nothing was there. It was empty. There was no life; no plants, no animals, no earth, nothing. Darkness was all you could see, it was on the face of the deep. The deep would be just a hole of darkness. God's Spirit was hovering over the face of the waters. Perhaps while He was hovering over it, he was planning what He would create in it. Planning how He could take nothing and make something out of it. Planning on how He would take darkness and make light.

Nothing happened in the darkness until God spoke. When God spoke, "Let there be light;" there was light. Think about how powerful God's word is. ***Nothing happened in this realm until God spoke it into existence.***

Hebrews: 11:1-3 Now faith is the substance of things hoped for, the evidence of things not seen. For by it the elders obtained a good testimony.

By faith we understand that the worlds were framed by the word of God, so that the things which are seen were not made of things which are visible.

The worlds were framed by the word of God. Everything that you see was not made by things which are visible; in other words, by things in this carnal realm. It was all made by the word of God. God spoke His word and creation happened; just like an artist that places his brush on his palette, mixes the colors and paints the most beautiful scene, so God strokes his palette of complete darkness with His word, to create a magnificent masterpiece filled with the heavens, the earth, the seas, grass, herbs, trees, the stars, the moon, the sun, every living sea creature, the birds, beasts of the field, every creeping thing and man.

There is a divine order and a plan in this universe. The laws of nature and the laws of science come together. There is a wisdom so awesome, so much higher than our ways that we can't comprehend it in our finite minds. No big bang theory could even come close to putting into motion this wonderful universe that we experience everyday.

So, God spoke into existence everything that we see. He turned that darkness into beautiful light with His spoken Word.

The same Spirit of the living God lives in each of us, and nothing is going to change in our darkness until we learn to speak into it. The Lord did not leave us defenseless to grope in the darkness. He gave us His word; and in His word is the answer to every problem that we face, every need that we have,

every promise that we are holding on to.
His word holds our blessings and our victories.
His word defeats our enemies.
There is nothing more powerful that you can speak out than His Word.

NOTHING HAPPENED IN THE DARKNESS UNTIL GOD SPOKE INTO IT. AND NOTHING IS GOING TO HAPPEN IN YOUR DARKNESS UNTIL YOU BEGIN TO SPEAK INTO IT!

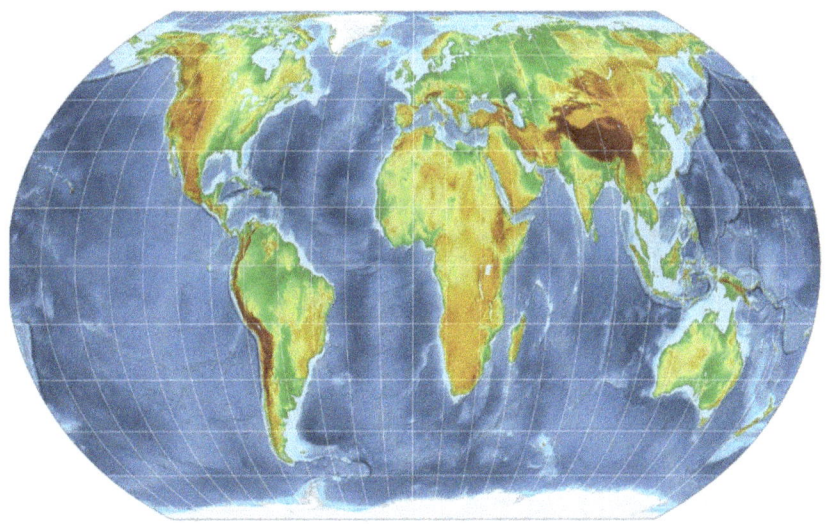

This Photo by Unknown Author is licensed under CC BY-SA

Hebrews 4:12 For the word of God is living and powerful, and sharper than any two-edged sword, piercing even to the division of soul and spirit, and of joints and the marrow and is a discerner of the intents of the heart.

For the word of God to be living and powerful and sharper than any two-edged sword that it could **pierce** the division of soul and spirit and the joints and marrow ….**it has to be spoken!** To pierce means to pass through or into. It means to stab, make a hole, perforate, break through. It is something that has to go forth.

Piercing involves engaging one element with another.

THE SWORD OF THE SPIRIT

Chapter 17 Bible Study:

1. What did God do to change the darkness into light?

2. How were the worlds formed?

3. Where can we find the answers for everything we need?

4. What has to happen to the word of God in order for it to be living, powerful and sharper than the two-edge sword?

5. Once you speak the word of God, it now becomes what?

CHAPTER 18

IT IS THE SPOKEN WORD OF GOD WHICH ENGAGES THE BATTLE!

You can know the Bible inside and out and have God's word hidden in your heart but unless you speak it out it will not change your darkness. Let me repeat that, **unless you speak it out, it will not change your darkness.** We have our part to do in this spiritual warfare. Jesus fights our battle for us, but we must engage it. He can do nothing until we engage it. The angels of the Lord are in stand by mode, waiting for someone to engage the battle. Jesus wants to help us, but He can't until someone engages the battle.

When we speak God's word out, it now becomes our Sword of the Spirit! The spoken word of God, the Sword of the Spirit is what engages the battle!

This is where I feel a lot of churches come up short. They do not teach on engaging the battle. This is crucial to bringing blessings into our lives. This is the difference in having a victorious life or not. So what can we speak out that will send Satan on his heels? There are many examples in the 'The word of God', the Bible. But the first strategic weapon that I teach a new believer in Christ is 'The Name of Jesus.'

THE NAME OF JESUS

Philippians 2: 5-11 says: Let this mind be in you which was also in Christ Jesus, who, being in the form of God, did not consider it robbery to be equal with God, but made Himself of no reputation, taking the form of a servant, and coming in the likeness of men. And being found in appearance a man, He humbled himself and became obedient to the point of death, even the death of the cross. Therefore God also has highly exalted him and given Him the name which is above every name, that at the name of Jesus

every knee should bow, of those in heaven, and of those on earth, and of those under the earth, and that every tongue should confess that Jesus Christ is Lord, to the glory of God the Father.

The first weapon that I teach a new believer in Christ, is the name of Jesus. At the name of Jesus every demon will flee. There is no other name that a demon or Satan will flee from. It is so powerful that every knee in heaven, on earth and beneath the earth will bow. It is the only name that a man can call upon and be saved. There is no other name. Jesus said whatever we ask in His name it will be done by our Father in heaven. Why is the name of Jesus so powerful? Because Jesus did what no one else would do, or could do. He took our place on Calvary and shed His blood for the sins of the world. He paid the ultimate sacrifice. He is the only one who did it. It wasn't a church who died for you. It wasn't a religion that died for you. It wasn't a man, a particular prophet or a religious leader……it was Jesus! Therefore, God the Father has highly exalted Him and given Him a name that is above every name.

So why would you pray to anyone else? He has the highest name in the universe!

As soon as you speak out the name of Jesus, Jesus shows up. You might not see Him in this carnal realm, but He is there. He is the best body guard a person can have. Just think, no matter what situation you are in, He shows up at the mention of His name. Jesus also said in **Matthew 18:19-20 "Again I say to you that if two of you agree on earth concerning anything that they ask, it will be done for them by my Father in heaven. For where two or three are gathered together in My name, I am there in the midst of them."**

So, when you come together for prayer or a church service, Jesus is there. Isn't it comforting to know that He says, 'I will never leave you or forsake you, I am with you always.' When I pray bed time prayers with little ones, I teach them that they don't have to be afraid of the dark. All they have to do is mention the name of Jesus and any fear or darkness has to go.

What a wonderful Savior we have. Just the mention of Jesus' name and Satan will flee from you.

THE BLOOD OF JESUS

The first mention that blood was spilled in the Bible is Genesis 3:21, when the Lord made tunics of skin to clothe Adam and his wife Eve, because of their sin of disobedience when they ate from the Tree of Knowledge of Good and Evil.

Because of sin, death has now entered in, and man lost his life, animals lost their life and plants lost their life. So the fig leaves that Adam and Eve sewed together to cover their nakedness would be of no use; for they would die, dry up and fall off of them. Their nakedness would still be uncovered.

The Lord had to kill an animal to cover their nakedness. Only a tunic of skin could cover them. Therefore, the blood had to be spilled, which means a sacrifice had to be made for their sin. An animal had to lose its life, to pay for the sin. So blood is the atonement for sin. Atonement means satisfaction given for wrong-doing. It means to make amends.

When the Lord instituted the 'Passover' in chapter 12 of Exodus, He commanded the congregation of Israel on the tenth of this month, every man shall take for himself a lamb, according to the house of his father. And the lamb shall be without blemish, a male of the first year. And they shall kill it at twilight and take some of the blood and put it on the two door posts and on the lintel of the houses.

Reading from verse 12: **For I will pass through the land of Egypt on that night, and will strike all the first born in the land of Egypt, both man and beast; and against all the gods of Egypt I will execute judgment; I am the Lord. Now the blood shall be a sign for you on the houses where you are. And when I see the blood. I will pass over you; and the plague shall not be on you to destroy you when I strike the land of Egypt.**

In this passage we see that the *'blood'* on the door posts and lintels is a sign for the Lord to pass over and the people of that house would not endure the judgments of the Lord. All the people in the house would be saved. So a lamb had to be killed, a sacrifice made, and the blood put on the door posts and lintels as a sign to the Lord that the sacrifice was made and the blood had been applied.

When Moses wrote all the laws and statues in **'The Book of the Covenant'**, he took the blood of animals that were sacrificed and sprinkled it on the altar and the people, and said, "This is the blood of the covenant which the Lord has made with you according to all these words." So here, the blood represents a covenant between us and the Lord.

But the blood of calves, goats and sheep which they offered continually year by year could never make those who approach the altar perfect. For those sacrifices are a reminder of sins every year. Reading from **Hebrews 10:5-7,9 Therefore when He came into the world, He said; "Sacrifice and offerings You did not desire, but a body You have prepared for Me. In burnt offerings and sacrifices for sin You had no pleasure. Then I said, 'Behold, I have come-In the volume of the book it is written of Me-To do Your will, O God.'"**

He takes away the first that He may establish the second. By that, we have been sanctified through the offering of the body of Jesus Christ once for all.

Hebrews 11:10-14 And every priest stands ministering daily and offering repeatedly the same sacrifices, which can never take away sins. But this Man, after He had offered one sacrifice for sins forever, sat down at the right hand of God, from that time waiting till His enemies are made His footstool. For by one offering He has perfected forever those who are being sanctified.

So, why is Satan afraid of the 'blood'? Because the 'blood' represents the atonement, the sacrifice for sins. Through the 'blood' of the Lamb (Jesus) we are forgiven and have eternal life. The blood of the Lamb is the 'New Covenant'.

Satan will flee from the 'blood' of the Lamb. He hates the blood. When you are praying cover your requests with the 'blood' of the Lamb and Satan won't be able to touch your prayers.

BINDING AND LOOSING

As mentioned in a previous chapter on the Keys of the Kingdom, in Matthew chapter 16, Jesus told Peter that because he knew who He was that He was going to give him the keys of the kingdom, and whatever he binds on earth would be bound in heaven, and whatever he loose from earth would be loosed from heaven. Jesus also talks about binding and loosing in Matthew Chapter 18:18-20.

We will find it again reading from **Matthew 12:22-30** A man was brought to Jesus who was demon-possessed, blind and mute. Jesus healed him and the multitudes questioned, "Could this be the Son of David?" But the religious leaders, the Pharisees said, "This fellow does not cast out demons except by Beelzebub, the ruler of the demons." But Jesus knew their thoughts and said to them: **"Every kingdom divided against itself is brought to desolation, and every city or house divided against itself will not stand. If Satan casts out Satan, he is divided against himself. How then will his kingdom stand?**

And if I cast out demons by Beelzubub, by whom do your sons cast them out? Therefore they shall be your judges. But if I cast out demons by the Spirit of God, surely the kingdom of God has come upon you. Or else how can one enter a strong man's house and plunder his goods, unless he first binds the strong man? And then he will plunder his house. He who is not with Me is against Me, and he who does not gather with Me scatters abroad."

The strong man is Satan. The goods that he has belongs to us. **We cannot plunder his goods unless we first bind the strong man.** Plunder his goods means to take by force or to rob. Why would the Bible tell us to rob someone or take by force his goods? Because, they belong to us. Satan has stolen our goods; our peace, our finances, our happiness, our relationships. He has our goods! Jesus said that the thief does not come except to steal, kill and destroy. He wants to steal everything from us, he would like to kill us and then destroy us in hell with him forever. So how do we bind the devil and his demons if we can't see him?

How do we fight him when he is in the spiritual realm and we are in the carnal realm?

The ANSWER……..THE SPOKEN WORD OF GOD!

Whenever we speak out, *'I bind you Satan in the name of the Lord Jesus Christ,'* immediately angels are dispatched to bind the devil's hands and take him out into outer darkness. How do I know this? In Matthew chapter 22, Jesus said the kingdom of heaven is like a certain king who arranged a marriage for his son and sent his servants out to call those who were invited to the wedding.

But some of those who were invited were not willing to come. They all had excuses and the king was furious, so reading from verse 8-14. **"Then he said to his servants, 'The wedding is ready, but those who were invited were not worthy. Therefore go into the highways, and as many as you find, invite to the wedding.' So those servants went out into the highways and gathered together all whom they found, both bad and good. And the wedding hall was filled with guests. But when the king came in to see the guests, he saw a man there who did not have on a wedding garment. So he said to him, 'Friend, how did you come in here without a wedding garment?' And he was speechless. Then the king said to the servants, 'Bind him hand and foot, take him away, and cast him into outer darkness; there will be weeping and gnashing of teeth.' "For many are called, but few are chosen."** Here we see a man who is not saved, does not have a wedding garment on, and the king's servants bind him and cast him into outer darkness. This is what happens when we say, 'I bind you devil in the name of the Lord Jesus Christ', angels come into our situation and take hold of the devil and bind him (place chains around him) and cast him away from your situation.

This is important for Jesus mentions it three times in the book of Matthew; chapter 12, chapter 16 and chapter 18.
Jesus would not have mentioned it three times in one gospel if He didn't want us to take notice. So, whenever something bad is coming against us, we have the authority to bind the
powers of darkness that is behind every struggle that we face. We have the authority to stop Satan and his demons in their tracks. We don't have to put up with the chaos. Jesus said in
Luke 10:18-19 And He said to them, "I saw Satan fall like lightning from heaven. Behold, I give you the authority to trample on serpents and scorpions, and over all the power of the enemy, and nothing shall by any means hurt you."
We have the authority through Jesus Christ to trample on serpents and scorpions. We have the authority. Now if only we would take up the authority and use it.

When we want to call blessings into our situation, we loosen that from heaven. Jesus said whatever we loosen on earth is loosened in heaven. So here we can loosen things that we need or want; like finances, health, blessings, peace, relationships etc. So, whatever you are praying for, for example, just say 'I loosen from heaven more peace in my life in Jesus's mighty Name.' Amen.

Speaking out the word 'bind' in the spiritual realm is the way to not only bind the enemy out of our situation but to cast him out into outer darkness so he can't come back. **Remember the enemy will flee from the name of Jesus. He will flee from the blood of Jesus, but he won't be bound and cast out until ……………..YOU BIND HIM!**

Chapter 18 Bible Study:

1. What engages the battle?

2. When we speak out the spoken Word of God, it now becomes_____.

3. What name is above every name?

4. What does atonement mean?

5. When blood is spilled for an offense, what is it called?

6. What had to be placed on the door posts and lintel of a house for the Lord to pass over?

7. Who is the strong man in Matthew chapter 12?

8. We cannot plunder the strong man's goods except we do what?

9. What is dispatched into our situation as soon as we say, 'I bind you devil in Jesus' name?

10. The enemy will flee from the blood of Jesus and the name of Jesus, but he won't be bound and cast out into outer darkness until what?

Chapter 19

Engaging the Battle….FAITH

<u>Genesis 3:14-15</u> So the Lord God said to the serpent:

> "Because you have done this,
>
> You are cursed more than all cattle,
>
> And more than every beast of the field;
>
> On your belly you shall go,
>
> And you shall eat dust
>
> All the days of your life.
>
> And I will put enmity
>
> Between you and the woman,

And between your seed and

her Seed; (her Seed is Jesus)

He shall bruise your head,

(He.. is Jesus)

And you shall bruise His heel."

The battle began when the serpent beguiled Eve and received the curse. It would continue between the seed of the serpent and the seed of the woman until the end of time. Though Satan would bruise our heels Jesus gets ultimate victory and bruises his head!

Revelation 20:10 The devil, who deceived them, was cast into the lake of fire and brimstone where the beast and the false prophet are. And they will be tormented day and night forever and ever.

Stay with Jesus Saints, for He WINS!

[This Photo](#) by Unknown Author is licensed under [CC BY-NC-SA](#)

FAITH

Hebrew 11:1-3 Now faith is the substance of things hoped for, the evidence of things not seen. For by it the elders obtained a good testimony.

By faith we understand that the worlds were framed by the word of God, so that the things which are seen were not made of things which are visible.

11:6 But without faith it is impossible to please Him, for he who comes to God must believe that He is, and that He is a rewarder of those who diligently seek Him.

To have faith you must believe that He is. You must believe that God is real. That He is the head of the universe, and that nothing is impossible for Him. You must also believe that your efforts are not in vain. That He will reward you for your faithfulness, for persevering and believing in Him. But the key word here is diligently seeking Him. You must be determined. Don't give up. Keep persevering until that answer comes through.

<u>1 Samuel 17:2</u> And Saul and the men of Israel were gathered together, and they encamped in the Valley of Elah, and drew up in battle array against the Philistines.

A champion went out from the camp of the Philistines, named Goliath. Champion means a warrior who will fight in single combat as a stand-in for an entire army. Goliath stood nine feet, nine inches tall. He had a bronze helmet and a coat of mail that weighed about 125 pounds. He carried a huge spear, with its spear head weighing 17 pounds. He stood and cried out to the armies of Israel, and said to them, **1Samuel 17:8-11 "Why have you come out to line up for battle?**

Am I not a Philistine, and you the servants of Saul? Choose a man for yourselves, and let him come down to me. If he is able to fight with me and kill me, then we will be your servants. But if I prevail against him and kill him, then you shall be our servants and serve us. And the Philistine said, 'I defy the armies of Israel this day; give me a man, that we may fight together.' When Saul and all Israel heard these words of the Philistine, they were dismayed and greatly afraid."

David who came to bring supplies to his brothers, heard the words of this Philistine and asked, **"What shall be done for the man who kills this Philistine and takes away the reproach from Israel?"** He found out that the man who killed the Philistine would receive great riches; the king's daughter and his house would be exempted from taxes. And he said to Saul, **"Let no man's heart fail because of him; your servant will go and fight with this Philistine."** There are rewards for fighting and engaging the enemy of the Lord. Just as David would receive rewards, we also, when we are about our Father's business, will receive great rewards in this life and in the next.

In **Revelation chapter 22:12** Jesus says, **"And behold, I am coming quickly, and My reward is with Me, to give to everyone according to his work. I am the Alpha and the Omega, the beginning and the End, the First and the Last."**

His rewards are given out to those who are working for Him. The ones who are doing His commandments. Not just reading his commandments, not just knowing his commandments but doing them. Putting their faith into action.

1Samuel 17:33-37 And Saul said to David, "You are not able to go against this Philistine to fight with him; for you are a youth, and he a man of war from his youth."

But David said to Saul, "Your servant used to keep his father's sheep, and when a lion or a bear came and took a lamb out of the flock, I went out after it and struck it, and delivered the lamb from its mouth; and when it arose against me, I caught it by its beard, and struck and killed it.

Your servant has killed both lion and bear; and this uncircumcised Philistine will be like one of them, seeing he has defied the armies of the living God." Moreover David said, "The Lord, who delivered me from the paw of the lion and from the paw of the bear, He will deliver me from the hand of this Philistine."

David ran toward the army to meet the giant!

When David ran toward the enemy, he engaged the battle. This is where I feel that many Christians lose out on their victories because they fail to engage the battle. David didn't just sit around and wait for something good to happen.

He didn't rely on his brothers to get the job done. He didn't turn his back to the enemy and run. He didn't hope in his own strength to accomplish it. He did it, by trusting that the Lord was with him, and the battle belonged to Him. Though the battle belongs to the Lord, David had a part to do. He had to gather his stones from the brook, take up his sling shot, speak out his faith and run toward the enemy! And we have a part to do too. For the same God that was in David is in us. How do we do it? When we do spiritual warfare. When we put on the whole armor of God, equip ourselves with the weapons of warfare; pray in the spirit realm, speak out our faith, bind the enemy with God's word and cast him into outer darkness. Face the enemy head-on and run toward him.

David's faith was bigger than the enemy, because his faith was in the Lord God. He spoke his faith out, which became his Sword in the Spirit.

1Samuel 17:45-46 Then David said to the Philistine, "You come to me with a sword, with a spear, and with a javelin. But I come to you in the name of the Lord of host's, the God of the armies of Israel, whom you have defied.

This day the Lord will deliver you into my hand, and I will strike you and take your head from you. And this day I will give the carcasses of the camp of the Philistines to the birds of the air and the wild beasts of the earth, that all the earth may know that there is a God in Israel."

1Samuel 17:46 Then all this assembly shall know that the Lord does not save with sword and spear; for the battle is the Lord's, and He will give you into our hands."

1Samuel 17:48 And it was so, when the Philistine arose and came and drew near to meet David, that David hastened and ran toward the army to meet the Philistine.

James 4:7-10 Therefore submit to God. Resist the devil and he will flee from you. Draw near to God and He will draw near to you.

As David ran toward the enemy, he was pro-active. His attitude was determined to defeat this enemy with all of his strength, might and courage. He was fearless. His faith was in the God of Israel, whom previously helped him defeat a bear and a lion.

David also had a secret weapon. He had a stone in his bag, but this wasn't an ordinary stone. This stone represented a diety that is above all others. This stone represented the One who is the Almighty, the One who fights our battles, the One who defeated the enemy. This stone represented Jesus!

The stone that the builders rejected has become the chief cornerstone.

Chapter 19: Bible Study

1. When did the battle begin?

2. True of False: There are rewards for doing spiritual warfare.

3. What did David speak out before he ran toward the giant?

4. What did the stone represent in David's bag?

CHAPTER 20

A Stone and a Sling
Fervency in Warfare

Isaiah 28:16 Therefore thus says the Lord God:"Behold, I lay in Zion a stone for a foundation, A tried stone, a precious cornerstone a sure foundation; Whoever believes will not act hastily?

Luke 20:17 And He looked at them and said, "What then is this that is written; 'The stone that the builders rejected has become the chief cornerstone'. Whoever falls on that stone will be broken; but on whomever it falls, it will grind him to powder."

John 1:1 In the beginning was the Word, and the Word was with God, and the Word was God.

He was in the beginning with God.

John 1:14 And the Word became flesh and dwelt among us, and we beheld His glory, the glory as of the only begotten of the Father, full of grace and truth.

STONE=JESUS=WORD OF GOD

1 Samuel 17:49-50 Then David put his hand in his bag and took out a stone; and he slung it and struck the Philistine in his forehead, so that the stone sank into his forehead, and he fell on his face to the earth.

So David prevailed over the Philistine with a sling and a stone, and struck the Philistine and killed him. But there was no sword in the hand of David.

The stone represents Jesus which is the Word of God. But the important part here is that David slung the stone with all of his might. He put all of his faith and strength in the Lord as he slung the stone. And we, when we believe with all of our heart, soul, mind and strength that Jesus will fight for us, and we engage the battle with such fervency no demon or devil in hell will be able to stand against us, for Jesus fights the battle, but we have to do our part and engage it! The more fervent we are, the more we get Jesus' attention and the more He fights and sends out His angels to fight for us.

The Sling represents - fervency when speaking out God's Word!

James 5:16 Confess your trespasses to one another, and pray for one another, that you may be healed. The effective, fervent prayer of a righteous man avails much.

The word fervent means 1. Hot; burning; glowing. 2. Having or showing great warmth of feeling; intensely earnest.

When you decide that you are sick and tired of the enemy defeating you in your relationships, finances, happiness and health; and you are ready to take back what the devil stole from you and mean it with everything in your spirit man, no demon of hell can stop you.

The more fervent you are, the more you get Jesus' attention. He showed me in prayer that it is the fervency in warfare that gets results. When you pray with great fervency, the prayers boil the waters in the River of Life before the throne of God. When the waters of the river are boiling you get Jesus' attention. He comes off His throne and scoops the bubbles up with a pail, sits down and looks intently at each prayer request in the bubbles. He sees the faces of the people you are praying for, He then answers the prayer, sends forth His mighty angels to undertake the situation and blows the bubbles out into the universe.

Jesus knew what it meant to be fervent in prayer. **Luke 22:39-46**

And coming out, He went to the Mount of Olives, as He was accustomed, and His disciples also followed Him. When He came to the place, He said to them, "Pray that you may not enter into temptation." And He was withdrawn from them about a stone's throw, and He knelt down and prayed, saying, "Father, if it is Your will, remove this cup from Me; nevertheless not My will, but Yours, be done."

Then an angel appeared to Him from heaven, strengthening Him. And being in agony, He prayed more earnestly. And His sweat became like great drops of blood falling down to the ground. When He arose up from prayer, and had come to His disciples, He found them sleeping from sorrow. Then He said to them, "Why do you sleep? Rise and pray, lest you enter into temptation."

James 5:17 Elijah was a man with a nature like ours, and he prayed earnestly that it would not rain; and it did not rain on the land for three years and six months. And he prayed again, and the heaven gave rain, and the earth produced its fruit.

In the book of Jeremiah, the Lord mentions a boiling pot. **In verse13 of chapter 1**, it reads, **And the word of the Lord came to me the second time, saying, "What do you see?" And I said, "I see a boiling pot, and it is facing away from the north." Then the Lord said to me: "Out of the north calamity shall break forth on all the inhabitants of the land. For behold, I am calling all the families of the kingdoms of the north," says the Lord;

They shall come and each one set his throne at the entrance of the gates of Jerusalem, against all its walls all around, and against all the cities of Judah. I will utter My judgements against them concerning all their wickedness, because they have forsaken Me, burned incense to other gods, and worshiped the works of their own hands."

So here: the boiling pot represents God's judgments being poured out on the people for their wickedness. When we are praying for someone or some situation to change in our life or our family and we are so fervent about it that we are boiling the waters of the river of life, that boiling pot that the Lord takes out of the waters with your prayer requests will go forth with the blessings and judgments of the Lord. You will see things happen! Lives will be changed because someone cares, someone is interceding. The enemy will be defeated. You will also be rewarded for pursuing the enemy.

The Boiling Pot in the River of Life

COMBINE THE ARMOR AND WEAPONS ON A SOLDIER THAT IS TOTALLY SUBMITTED AND YOU WILL HAVE ONE POWERFUL SWORD OF THE SPIRIT!

THE WAR IS ON

Matt: 11:12 And from the days of John the Baptist until now the kingdom of heaven suffers violence, and the violent take it by force.

Jesus is speaking and He makes a statement that the violent take the kingdom by force. The winning side is the one that is most violent in the spiritual realm. How much do you want to see breakthroughs in your life? Are you willing to fight for them? Will you take the time and engage the battle. Will you mean it with all of your heart, soul, mind, spirit and strength? Will you be persistent, steadfast and determined to plunder the enemy?

We know that the enemy is very wicked and cunning. He will go to any extent to rob us from our blessings, try to kill us and then destroy us in hell with him forever. Jesus says in **John 10:10 "The thief does not come except to steal, and to kill and to destroy.**

I have come that they may have life, and that they may have it more abundantly". Notice, that Jesus said *may* have, because it is **up** to us rather or **not** we will have a more abundant life. Are you willing to fight in the spirit realm until you get the victory? You have to be more violent than the enemy. The more fervent you are, the more determined, the more persistent, the greater the victories!

James 5:14 The effective, fervent prayer of a righteous man avails much.

Chapter 20 Bible Study:

1. Who is the stone that the builder's rejected?

2. When David slung the stone with all of his might, what did this represent?

3. What happens in the river of life with you pray with much fervency?

4. Who picks up the boiling pot and answers the prayers?

5. Who is the winning side that takes the kingdom of heaven?

CHAPTER 21

THE THREE HEAVENS

Paul writing in 2 Corinthians chapter 12 said that he knew a man in Christ who was caught up to the third heaven. He was caught up into Paradise and heard inexpressible words, which were not lawful for a man to utter. Paul is calling the 3rd heaven Paradise. Paradise is defined as any place or state of perfection, happiness. This must be where God's throne is.

Revelation 12:7 says, **And war broke out in heaven; Michael and his angels fought against the dragon; and the dragon and his angels fought, but they did not prevail, nor was a place found for them in heaven any longer.** We know there is no fighting in Paradise, for the Lamb is there. And Jesus, the Lamb of God; is the Prince of peace. So, this must be the second heaven. The second heaven is the place where angels and demons fight over our prayer requests.

Psalm 19:1 says **The heavens declare the glory of God; And the firmament shows His handiwork.** This is the realm in our atmosphere, where we can see the stars, the moon, sun etc. This has to be the first heaven.

In Daniel chapter 10, Daniel was fasting for 21 days seeking an answer for his prayer request when an angel appeared to him and spoke.

Reading from verse **11-14 And he said to me, "O Daniel, man greatly beloved, understand the words that I speak to you, and stand upright, for I have now been sent to you." While he was speaking this word to me, I stood trembling. Then he said to me, "Do not fear, Daniel, for from the first day that you set your heart to understand, and to humble yourself before your God, your words were heard; and I have come because of your words. But the prince of the kingdom of Persia with stood me twenty-one days; and behold, Michael, one of the chief princes, came to help me, for I had been left alone there with the kings of Persia.**

Now I have come to make you understand what will happen to your people in the latter days, for the vision refers to many days yet to come."

The prince of the kingdom of Persia is a demonic prince from Satan's kingdom. He fought with the angel sent to Daniel because he had the answer to his prayer. Michael, a chief prince in God's kingdom came to help him, and eventually he got through to Daniel. We see by these passages that the demons fight over our prayer requests. It is only our persistent prayer of faith that pulls the answer through the second heaven to our realm, the first heaven. Daniel did not give up. He was on his 21st day of fasting and praying.

Once we engage the battle, the Lord immediately puts his army into action; the angels are armed with swords, they mount up on horses, and they race into the battle.

They face the enemy head on; just like David did when he faced Goliath, he ran toward the enemy. They are fearless for they know who their captain is; **the captain of the host is Jesus!**

The more we pray with fervency and fury, the hotter the battle gets. We actually boil the River of Life with our prayers and prayer requests! When Jesus sees the river of life boiling, He gets off His throne and scoops a bucket of boiling water into a pail. He then takes out one bubble at a time, sees the face of the person we are praying for in the bubble, answers the prayer, by sending his angels out to fight the powers of darkness and then blows the bubble out into the universe.

Why is fervency so important? Because it gets Jesus' attention. When He sees the river of life boiling, He knows that the person praying is meaning it with all their heart and all of their strength. He knows that the person praying has faith in Him. Fervency sets off fire works in heaven. The armies of the Lord come to attention and are on high alert, knowing they are about to be sent out.

Fervency excites heaven! If you want to see things happen...then mean your prayers with all your heart and watch what happens!

Chapter 21 Bible Study:
1. **What is in the third heaven?**

2. **What heaven does the angels and demons fight in?**

3. **Where is the first heaven located?**

4. **Who tried to stop Daniel's prayer?**

5. **What pulls our prayers through the second heaven?**

CHAPTER 22

RETURN TO YOUR FIRST

When you first get saved, it is such a wonderful enlightening experience! Your whole world takes a 360 degree turn. Everything looks brighter and clearer. The peace and happiness you feel is worth more than all the riches in the world. Nothing compares with it.

The Lord wants you to stay with Him. He wants your fellowship, your love, your devotion. He wants to be your first love.

Jesus says in **Revelation 2:1-5 To the angel of the church of Ephesus write, These things says He who holds the seven stars in His right hand, who walks in the midst of the seven golden lampstands: "I know your works, your labor, your patience, and that you cannot bear those who are evil. And you have tested those who say they are apostles and are not, and have found them liars; and you have persevered and have patience, and have labored for My Name's sake and have not become weary.**

Nevertheless I have this against you, that you have left your first love. Remember therefore from where you have fallen; repent and do the first works, or else I will come to you quickly and remove your lampstand from its place unless you repent."

The Lord wants to be our first love. He wants to ***be first*** in our lives. He wants us to love Him before others. Whenever we fall in love with someone, don't we want to please them? We try to make them our best friend, buy them the best gifts, spend time with them, and confide in them our deepest secrets. They are the center of our universe. We lay our lives down to please them. This is the kind of devotion Jesus wants from us. This is the kind of love the Lord God Almighty deserves from us. Make Him first in your life and everything else will line up.

Now mount up Saints, take your rightful position in the Lord's army, pick up your Sword of the Spirit, engage the battle and watch Jesus trample those devils under your feet!

Revelation 19:13-16 He was clothed with a robe dipped in blood, and His name is called The Word of God. And the armies in heaven, clothed in fine linen, white and clean, followed Him on white horses. Now out of His mouth goes a sharp sword, that with it He should strike the nations. And He Himself will rule them with a rod of iron. He Himself treads the winepress of the fierceness and wrath of Almighty God. And he has on His robe and on His thigh a name written:

This Photo by Unknown Author is licensed under CC BY-NC-ND

KING OF KINGS AND LORD OF LORDS

Bible Studies Answers

Chapter 1:

1. His Spoken word
2. The Tree of Knowledge of good and evil
3. False
4. God
5. Lust of the flesh
   Lust of the eyes
   Pride of life
6. Death had now entered in
7. Blood had to be spilled, animal had to die
8. Jesus

Chapter 2:

1. Speaking God's Word

2. Because Satan will try to twist it and give us half-truths

3. To be like God, to be worshipped

4. Those who do the will of God

5. Believing in Jesus
6. That men loved darkness rather than light

Chapter 3:
1. Our relationship with the Lord
2. To provide and protect
3. He had already broken the first four, for his riches were before the Lord
4. Have them in the right order with the Lord first
5. Love the Lord your God with all your heart, soul and mind
6. Love your neighbor as yourself
7. Jesus
8. Only through Jesus

Chapter 4:
1. God with us
2. To save His people from their sins

3. Repent and believe the gospel
4. To fish for men
5. Lead people to Christ for salvation
6. Kingdom of God and His righteousness

Chapter 5:
1. Knowing who Jesus is
2. Powers of darkness coming against us.
3. Loosen good things; peace, happiness, finances etc.
4. The Anointed One
5. Be on the right side. Completely trust our Commander-in-Chief. Properly outfitted with our armor and weapons. And understanding the enemy

Chapter 6:
1. The whole armor of God
2. False

3. Shield of Faith
4. Helmet of Salvation

Chapter 7:
1. Be born again
2. He got baptized
3. Repent
4. True
5. True
6. Love, Joy, Peace, Longsuffering, Kindness, Goodness, Faithfulness, Gentleness and Self Control

Chapter 8:
1. Jesus
2. Yes
3. Jesus
4. God's word

Chapter 9:
1. Heart
2. To walk uprightly
3. Don't be married to an unbeliever
4. Holy Spirit

Chapter 10:
1. Get ready to go out with the Gospel
2. Read God's word and have it in your heart
3. Pray and abide in God's word
4. We can ask what we desire and it shall be done

Chapter 11:
1. Faith is the substance of things hoped for, the evidence of things not seen
2. No

3. The fiery darts of the enemy.
4. Must believe that He is and that He is a rewarder

Chapter 12:
1. Spiritual
2. Pull down strongholds, cast down arguments, bring every thought into captivity to the obedience of Christ, punish all disobedience
3. Total submission, Prayer & Fasting, Baptism of the Holy Spirit, Praise, Spoken Word of God, Faith and Fervency

Chapter 13:
1. Resist him, Steadfast in the faith
2. True
3. Yes
4. Be sober, be vigilant
5. Obedience, Love

6. Having love for one another.
7. Blessings

Chapter 14:
1. True
2. True
3. Denying the body, sacrifice, shows determination
4. 21 Days
5. Intimate time between you and the Father

Chapter 15:
1. Repent and be baptized
2. A camel carries burdens; He was pointing to the One that would carry our burdens
3. Honey represents ...the Word of God, Locusts represents ..the devourer
4. Jesus
5. Helper, Teacher, Comforter, Peace, Spirit of Truth
6. Power to be Jesus' disciples

Chapter 16:
1. Praise
2. Praise
3. Judah
4. God's presence
5. Sing and praise the Lord

Chapter 17:
1. He spoke into it
2. By God's spoken word
3. In God's word
4. Has to be spoken out
5. Sword of the Spirit

Chapter 18:
1. Spoken Word
2. Sword of the Spirit

3. Jesus
4. Satisfaction given for wrong doing... To make amends.
5. Sacrifice
6. Blood of the sacrifice
7. Satan
8. Bind him first
9. Angels
10. We bind him

Chapter 19:
1. Fall of man
2. True
3. His faith
4. God's Word = Jesus

Chapter 20:
1. Jesus
2. Fervency

3. Boil the waters

4. Jesus

5. The most violent

www.ingramcontent.com/pod-product-compliance
Lightning Source LLC
Chambersburg PA
CBHW071845080526
44589CB00012B/1119